D0432194

AMERICA'S PREMIER GUNMAKERS

REMINGTON

AMERICA'S PREMIER GUNMAKERS

REMINGTON

K.D. KIRKLAND

Published by World Publications Group, Inc.
140 Laurel Street
East Bridgewater, MA 02333
www.wrldpub.net

Reprinted 2008 by World Publications Group, Inc.
Copyright © 2007 World Publications Group, Inc.

ISBN 1-57215-103-X
978-1-57215-103-1

Printed and bound in China by
SNP Leefung Printers Limited

Designed by Ruth DeJauregui
Edited by Timothy Jacobs

Acknowledgements

The author extends his appreciation to Sylvia
Kirkland, Wayne Boyer and Dennis Clark of
Traders' Den in Logan, Utah. We would also
like to thank Ms Nola Clavio and Mr George K
Bukovsky of Remington Arms / E I du Pont de
Nemours & Co, Inc and Mr Mark A Sweetland
of Rumrill-Hoyt, Inc. The author and
publishers would also like to acknowledge the
book *Remington Arms, an American History*
by Alden Hatch, published in 1956 by
Rinehart & Company, Inc, from which much of
our historical information has been adapted.

Photo Credits

All photos courtesy of EI du Pont de Nemours
& Co, Inc except the following:

Bison Books 46
Cinema Shop 17, 40 (bottom), 89, 96–97
© RE DeJauregui 24, 74–75
EI du Pont de Nemours & Co, Inc via Rumrill-
    Hoyt 2–3 (all), 6–7, 10–11, 30–31, 90–91,
    94–95
Robert Hunt Picture Library 45 (bottom)
© KD Kirkland 10 (bottom), 86–87, 91
    (bottom), 92–93
National Archives 33 (all), 39
Peter Newark's Western Americana 35
    (bottom), 43, 58
Courtesy of Royal Artillery Institution,
    Museum of Artillery at the Rotunda, London
    Joseph Coughlan 35 (center)
Seaver Center for Western History Research,
    Natural History Museum of Los Angeles
    County 34–35, 38–39, 40–41 (top)
Smithsonian Institution 72 (bottom), 73 (all)
South Dakota State Historical Society 40–41
    (bottom)
United States Air Force 25
United States Army 47
United States Navy 42
Patty Warren's Antiques, Sacramento,
    California 67, 68, 69, 70 (all), 71
© Bill Yenne 99

Page one: A portrait of Eliphalet Remington II,
the man who began the Remington Arms company tradition at his father's foundry in Ilion,
New York.
Pages 2–3, top to bottom: Remington's high
quality is a tradition which is well-embodied in
these fine firearms: the 1100 Special Field
model is an autoloader with four-shot capacity
and a special gas metering system which
reduces recoil and improves accuracy; the
legendary Model 700 Mountain Rifle has a super
strong bolt action and is available in calibers up
to .300 Winchester Magnum; and the 870
Wingmaster model is a fine pump action with
five round capacity and the ingenious Rem
Choke interchangeable choke tubes, which is
like having several shotguns in one.
These pages, top to bottom: the Model 870
Wingmaster Deer Gun; the Model 870 20 gauge
Youth Gun; and the New Model 870 Express.

Table of Contents

A Remington

The Remington Parker shotgun shown *above* is one of the many reasons that Remington tops many gun collector's lists. This excellent side-by-side features good balance, light weight and great 'pointability.' Shown *below*, *from left to right* are some of this gem's finer points—Remington's fine engraving on the receiver; precision-made breech components; and evidence that Remington workmanship continues right down to and including the buttstock. Note the designs which adorn even the screws and screwholes here!

History

A history of the Remington Arms Company is a miniature panorama of American history itself. In 1816, on the heels of the War of 1812, Eliphalet Remington and his son, Eliphalet Jr, founded the Remington Company just outside of Ilion Gorge, New York.

Demand grew for the workmanship of the Remington father/son duo. Complete rifles were produced on a customized, individual basis, but profits were also to be had in producing barrels for other gunsmiths to be used in their own firearms. Increased demand always follows excellent workmanship, and the Remington business soon outgrew the production capacity of their original forge. In 1828, they moved their operation into Ilion proper, along the banks of the Erie Canal. The Canal at this time was the most important thoroughfare of commercial traffic in this region, and the new location proved to be successful indeed. The same year as the move to Ilion also brought tragedy. Eliphalet, Sr met an accidental death at this time.

The business expanded rapidly, and a year after the move, a second forge was installed to produce barrels, balls, and accessories. Because the Remingtons were selling principally to other gunsmiths, it is not uncommon to find REMINGTON markings on various *parts* of guns produced in this area during this period.

Eliphalet, Jr was now president of the company. He was a gunmaker and manufacturer first and foremost. While he was able to introduce many improvements in the fabrication of firearms and their accompanying parts, he is not remembered as a major innovator of the same genre as Samuel Colt, for example. Remington was a genius at combining the innovations and patents of others. Remington Arms was also a *production* facility, not particularly given to experimentation with untried ideas. So while blazing inventiveness was not a hallmark of Remington Arms, neither was the company dependent on just one invention or set of innovations for its continuing existence. In fact, Remington has one of the longest continuous histories of any US arms manufacturer.

Eventually, Eliphalet Jr's son Philo came into the family business, and the company changed its name to E Remington and Son. John Griffiths of Cincinnati had originally contracted with the US Government to produce 5000 Model 1841 Percussion 'Mississippi' Rifles. He was unable to fulfill his contract and the Remingtons took it over. This afforded them their first opportunity to produce, on a large scale, weapons for the government. Following this first contract, the government awarded the Remingtons a second contract for 7500 more of the same model. Remington had broken into the arms trade in a big way! In 1846–7, Remington also received a US Navy contract for the production of the Jenks Breech-loading Percussion Carbine. In 1851, another contract followed for the production of 7500 Model 1841 Percussion Rifles. By this time, demand was so great for their products that the Remingtons had expanded their manufacturing facilities to nearby Herkimer, New York. In the early 1850s, two more of Eliphalet, Jr's sons—namely, Samuel and Eliphalet III—entered the family business and E Remington and son was changed to E Remington and *Sons* to account for what was now a larger family partnership.

The Remingtons were not willing to confine themselves to the production of rifles and other long arms alone. Samuel Colt had patented his revolving percussion revolver in 1836, and a little over 20 years later—in 1857—the Remingtons introduced their Beals Pocket Revolvers. During the Civil War, Remington—along with all other arms manufacturers in the United States—devoted its complete time and resources to the fabrication of all sorts of firearms for the war effort.

Eliphalet Jr died in 1861, and his son Philo succeeded him as president of the firm. At the end of the Civil War, the company was reorganized as a corporation that retained the name of E Remington and Sons.

The Remington company played a significant role in the great American westward expansion. The company introduced a great variety of pistols and rifles. The most famous of their many lines of products was the 'Rolling Block' series of rifles. These were eagerly purchased by gun merchants both in the United States and abroad. Remington soon found itself squarely in the midst of a very lucrative stream of European contracts to upgrade the various armories of these nations. Samuel Remington died in 1882, and his brother Philo assumed full management of the company. In 1886, the company was in dire financial straits and went into receivership.

The company was acquired by Hartley and Graham in 1888. H and G was a famed New York military and sporting goods firm which had, twenty years earlier, founded the Union Metallic Cartridge Company of Bridgeport, Connecticut.

E Remington and Sons was renamed the Remington Arms Company and functioned as such from 1888 until 1912, when it was merged with the Union Metallic Cartridge Company. From then until 1934, the company was named Remington-UMC. The Great Depression brought yet another reorganization of the company and its name reverted to 'Remington Arms Company, Inc,' by which it is still known today. The DuPont Corporation acquired controlling interest in the firm in 1933.

Unlike other major American gun manufacturers, the definitive history-to-date of Remington Arms has yet to be fully written. There is really no fully documented chronological history of the company. Firearms collectors continue to have a very difficult time in cataloguing and tracing the numerous models and variations of Remington firearms. Often, manufacturing specifications would shift within the same model of gun without being documented by the factory, thus leaving collectors and dealers to surmise for themselves the details and peculiarities of whole lines of Remington products. The Remington Factory at times apparently overproduced, in anticipation of entering into contracts which never materialized. These inventories of parts were then salvaged by being used in other models for which

Below: **This Remington Sportsman 581 is just one of the fine rifles made by Remington, America's oldest sporting rifle manufacturer. The 581's five-shot capacity and rugged construction make it the ideal 'plinker.'** *At right:* **The Remington Arms plant at Ilion, in the 1940s.**

contracts did exist. Thus 'variations' within model runs are numerous and plaguing. Definitive technical data simply does not exist for many Remington models.

Tracing Remington's history as well as documenting model productions is for the most part a trip through uncharted waters. Gun collectors and historians are often at variance one with another as to production details concerning a particular model or variation on a model. These 'grey areas' of Remington history and production are both numerous and intriguing. They provide the historian and researcher with fertile, and sometimes frustrating, fields of endeavor. However, collectors have a difficult time establishing the rarity of certain models; this lends itself to confusions about value and the pricing of certain specimens.

It is interesting to note, also, that engraved Remingtons are somewhat rare. The only real engraving that was done at the factory was apparently on the Magazine Derringer Model. When engraving was done, it was usually very simple in form and basic in design. Most engraving is found on the early percussion handguns, but does not in any way compare to the engraving on contemporaneous Colts. When, however,

engraving was performed by Remington, it was accomplished by an acid etching process, in contrast to the rolled design made famous by Colt. Some engraved Remington longarms were produced but they are generally considered to be quite rare.

Boxed sets of Remington pistols are also considered rarities, because Remington Arms did not go in for exquisite presentation-grade specimens, as did some other American manufacturers. Remington did, however, employ 'specialty' grip materials in its production. Ivory and pearl were the most often used materials in Remington decorative grips. The value of a gun thus equipped is considered to generally be a function of its type—in conjunction with the *kind* of *grip material* employed and the overall *condition* of the firearm.

Today, Remington produces numerous lines of both sporting and military weapons. Remington Arms are found at all 'wavelengths' of the firearms spectrum. Remington does offer superb finish and fine wood (and other) stocks. The longest-lasting American gun manufacturer continues to uphold its tradition of offering the public well-made, accurate and superbly finished weapons for a fair price.

Civilian

Above: The Remington Model 700 hunting rifle. *At right:* Montanans Thayne Bowman (white shirt) and Tom Yule (plaid jacket) and their Remington Mohawk .222s, equipped with Leopold scopes, and Tom's son Tim with his Bushnell Sportview 4x-equipped Mohawk.

Arms

Non-military use of firearms generally falls into the categories of hunting and target shooting. Conservation has come to characterize the first group and national and international competitions have come to characterize the second category.

The Remington Arms Company has played a significant role in both of these areas of civilian firearms use. One of the hallmarks of Remington guns is that they are priced for availability. Probably a greater percentage of firearms in private hands in the Unites States are of Remington make than of any other manufacturer. Remingtons are functional, reliable and tend to maintain their value.

Rifles

Firearms literature abounds with never-ending debates about what constitutes the 'perfect' rifle. This debate tends to center around a balance between two points. The first is the caliber desired (which itself tends toward a 'perfection' of its own) and the second is the rifle itself. Choosing a firearm for personal use requires that the purchaser has in mind beforehand the use to which the gun will be put. This involves such considerations as whether one wants exclusively to shoot targets, or shoot *and* go hunting for game, or wants to hunt exclusively; also, if shooting targets, at what ranges and distances will one be shooting, and will it be serious competition shooting; and if hunting, what sort of game and what sort of habitat does this game prefer—and so on. Does one require long range accuracy or does what one would be doing call for sheer muzzle power? The type of action of the gun must also be taken into account; also, the 'convenience' of a rifle—that is, its weight and handling

capabilities—are of prime importance in the selection process. The more forethought that is put into choosing a rifle, the greater will be the satisfactions of using that gun in the future.

Probably, the most popular rifle caliber is the .30-06, a caliber that has bagged more brown bears and grizzlies than any other caliber of this century. It is available in a wide variety of bullet styles and weights. Almost all rifle mechanism types are available in .30-06 caliber with the exception of a few lever-actions. While it is true that, technically speaking, no caliber of rifle is 'perfect,' the .30-06 comes about as close as one can come to perfection in an imperfect world.

After World War II, one of the more interesting innovations that occurred in the American gunmaking industry was the introduction of Monte Carlo stocks. The Monte Carlo comb, when incorporated into a stock design, raises the mid part of the stock sufficiently to cause one's cheek to rest at a higher position when looking down the sights. Remington began producing Monte Carlo stocks for many of its models. Firearms writers and critics both raved about and reviled the Monte Carlo design. Some claimed that it reduced perceived recoil when the rifle was fired. Others claimed (and rightfully so) that the Monte Carlo comb actually *increases* perceived recoil. Actually, the Monte Carlo design was simply a way of skirting the inherent design problems of pre-World War II stocks without actually doing anything about them. When soldiers began returning from World War II, their demands on their hunting rifles were greater than before the war. Battlefield experience yielded more sophisticated thinking about what they actually wanted out of their rifles.

Most everyone in this period wanted telescopic sights; but telescopic sights and the old stock designs were not an easy match. The Monte Carlo design at first seemed to come to the rescue, offering a higher cheek position—and thus better eye access to 'scopes'—than the old stocks did. So the band wagon was set into motion, and Remington, along with most other manufacturers, began making Monte Carlo stocks available on their most prominent models.

By the middle-to-late 1970s the Monte Carlo fad had pretty much run its course. In the early 1970s, even before this turn of events, Remington contacted Jim Carmichael—who is generally acknowledged as the dean of modern gun writers—with a request that he design a classic-styled stock for the Model 700 bolt action rifle. Carmichel says that designing the stock was something of an exercise in frustration, but the Model 700 Classic was a result of his labors. The Model 700 Classic certainly looks better than Remington's old Monte Carlo stocks and actually feels better to shoot. This Remington innovation—that of designing a 'classic' stock—forced other gunmakers to follow suit. The 'classic design' has by now superseded the Monte Carlo in most respects. It actually solves the pre-World War II stock design problems by supplying the higher comb needed for telescopic sight shooting *and* eliminates many of the undesirable features of the Monte Carlo design. 'Classic' stocks feature a straight, high comb and reduce perceived recoil. In addition, they generally look a great deal better than Monte Carlos.

Remington had been active in production of weapons for World War I, but with peace in 1918 and the Great Depression of the 1930s, demand virtually dried up for Remington products. The factory at Ilion continued to exist, but shipments of products were few and this period produced considerable losses for the company. During this time, Remington's profitably was mainly due to its cartridge division in Bridgeport. Despite the overall depressed economic circumstances, the DuPont Corporation saw an opportunity in Remington, and purchased controlling interest of the firm in 1933. At this time, Remington was running third in the American arms market behind Winchester and Savage. DuPont's original intention was to close the firearms division of the business and concentrate wholly on the cartridge division. But before doing so, company policy dictated that a survey be taken of the firearms division before closure. George Read was sent from DuPont of Wilmington to Ilion for this purpose. Read would later recommend that the firearms division not be dissolved but rather upgraded and modernized. DuPont followed through by pumping investment dollars into Ilion. New equipment was acquired, fabrication processes were set up, and attempts were made to modernize the whole manufacturing process.

During this time, the most popular bolt action rifle on the market was the Winchester Model 70. Remington undertook to compete with the Model 70 by introducing the Remington Model 720 in 1941. The Model 720 was indeed competitive with Winchester but in 1941 the United States was forced into a war not of its own making. The production of sporting arms was simply set aside for the now immediate problem of emergency war production. It is interesting to note, however, that while Remington

was blessed with huge arms contracts from the government for World War II, these contracts resulted in very meager profits for the company. This is an example of a little known historic fact: Arms manufacturers do not generally profit from war.

During World War I, Congress had determined that no manufacturer or transportation agency would engage in war profiteering. When World War II fell upon the nation, Congress was once again determined that windfall profits were to be kept at a minimum. But Remington's factories and facilities had to be expanded and tooled up for the increased war production. This overbuilding and excessive expansion could prove disastrous for Remington after the war was over. DuPont management realized this and undertook an extensive 'Reconversion and Modernization' program to utilize the expanded facilities of the company after the

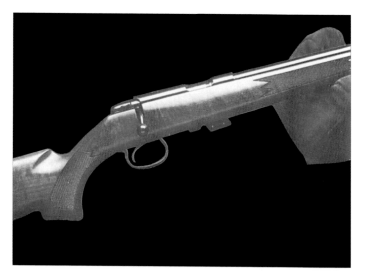

At right: The Remington Model 541T bolt action rimfire rifle. Model 700 rifles feature hunting calibers and a variety of types. *Above, from the top down:* The Model 700 Mountain Rifle, the Model 700 BDL with Monte Carlo stock and the Model 7 lightweight 700 variant. *Below:* A close look at a Remington Model 700 Mountain Rifle.

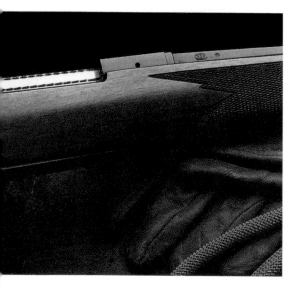

war, and thus insure its continued existence. At the heart of this project was the design and fabrication of the Model 721 and 722 rifles. These rifles had to succeed or Remington Firearms itself would cease to exist.

When crucial times arrived, crucial personalities arose. Mike Walker became the driving force behind the production of the new rifles. Walker hailed from Iowa and had answered an ad in the American Rifle magazine in 1942 when Remington was searching for research engineers. Remington was gathering its engineering talent at this time in order to meet the intensive wartime production schedule. This pool of talent would later prove indispensable to the success of the company. Technically, the Model 721/722 rifle project began on 12 August 1942, when $200 was authorized to prepare a project outline. In 1943, the

research and development department spent $11,500 for background research—but it was not until almost at war's end that the project was again a priority.

In August of 1944, Walker was placed at the head of the 721/722 project and given $35,000 to begin building prototypes for the new rifles. Walker headed a team of designers which was remarkably small for what was to become such a major weapon project: only three men—Dana McNally, Leon Rix and Knute Reed—were assigned to produce the drawings and fabricate the prototype form.

The feasibility studies that had been done in 1942 established the rough parameters of what the 721/722 rifles should be. These parameters stated that the rifles should be light in weight and fast handling; their production costs must be low enough to provide sufficient profitably for the company; they would have to be capable of being manufactured with mass-production techniques; and the new rifles were not to compete head to head with the Winchester Model 70, but rather were to eat into the Winchester Model 94, Marlin Model 86 and Savage Model 40 markets. The fascinating thing about the model 721/722 project is that it brought to bear a sectional talent in such a way that the rifles that were produced are, even today, bench marks in the production history of center fire weapons. In terms of productivity, the Model 721 rifle only required 60 machine operations, whereas its predecessor, the Model 720, required 250 such operations. Here was efficiency indeed! Because of the unique production processes involved, precision parts could be produced without the high degree of individual workmanship previously needed.

The original 721/722 design drawings called for the rifles to be produced in four barrel lengths ranging from 20 to 26 inches. However, production models were actually produced in 24 and 26 inch lengths. Later 22-inch barrels were offered for some calibers. The 721/722 weighed only 7.25 pounds at the most. By comparison, Winchester's Model 70 weighed 7.75 pounds and most of Remington's other competitors

14

weighed in at a hefty eight pounds or more. Standard stocks for the 721/722 were cut from American walnut and featured a standard pistol grip with a semi-beavertail forearm; and the two basic stock designs were the iron sight version—which dropped 1.87 inches at the comb and 2.87 inches at the heel—and a high comb stock which dropped 1.38 inches at the comb and 2.19 inches at the heel.

The 721/722s were marketed in five chamberings: .30-06, .270 Winchester, .300 H and H Magnum, .257 Roberts and .300 Savage. The 220 Swift was originally planned for the 721 rifle but was dropped in favor of the Remington .222 cartridge. The .222 Remington is still of universal popularity today as a fine varmint caliber. The introduction of the .222 Remington greatly enhanced the sales of the short-action 722 rifles. In time, other calibers became available for the Model 721, namely the .280 Remington, the .264 Winchester Magnum, the .308 Winchester, the .244 Remington, the .222 Remington Magnum and the .243 Winchester.

The series of tests to which the 721/722 rifles were subjected were extensive almost beyond belief. Various cold, rain, dust and endurance tests were devised. Ice tests and blow-up tests were later added. Machinery was set up to subject the rifles to 50,000-round firings in order to check the wear on the bolt and firing systems. Even gas leak tests were conducted in an 'iron lung' type of device. These last tests were meant to determine safety parameters beyond those generally encountered by hunters. The blow-up tests were by far the most publicized. These tests were conducted in the .30-06 caliber, which was considered to be potentially the most dangerous load fired through the 721/722 rifles. No fewer than five 220-grain cartridges were lodged into the rifles one after the other, and then the weapon was fired. Remington estimated that the internal pressures thus created exceeded 300,000 pounds per square inch. This was testing taken to extraordinary lengths, but it did provide the company with excellent advertising and valuable data concerning the strength of the new actions.

Remington had a fine product, but still had to convince the United States patent office that no one else's patents were being stepped on by this new product. The company's lawyers had to produce written depositions that established when, where and who

At left: The Model 700 is world renowned for its accuracy and strength. Available in 16 calibers, this big game rifle features handcrafted fit and finish—as is implied by this photograph. *Below:* The potent Remington 660 Carbine with sling and shock pad, and *below left*, without same.

actually worked on the new rifles. The patent people in Washington wanted to examine all of the blow-up test specimens as well as Remington's competitor's specimens.

The 721/722 project was kept a virtual secret at the factory. In the spring of 1947, rumors were surfacing of a new Remington product. At this time, some writers were actually shown the first prototype specimens. They immediately recognized that here were entirely new rifle designs, not just remakes composed of spare military parts. The official announcements were made and actual marketing began in January 1948.

The 721s and 722s were first marketed at more expensive prices than had been originally planned. The 721 retailed for around $80.00 and the 722 for around $75.00. By this time, the Winchester 94 sold for about $60.00 and the Marlin Model 86 went for about $59.00. The purchaser of the Remingtons paid a little more, but got impressively much more. This fact actually made the $110.00 price tag on the Winchester Model 70 seem expensive in comparison to what the buyer was actually getting for his money. The 721/722s were in fact just as good as the Winchester Model 70s at considerably less cost. Many shooters during this period had actually become accustomed to paying upwards of $200.00 for custom rifles built from surplus military parts. Thus a truly fine $80.00 rifle with state-of-the-art performance was a welcome and eagerly sought-after piece of merchandise. Deliveries of various calibers began in 1948 with the .30-06

Springfield coming out in March of that year, followed by the .300 Savage in May, the .270 Winchester and .250 Roberts in July, and, finally, the .300 H and H Magnum in September. Two grades of the rifle were made—the standard and the fancy. The fancy grade was subdivided into various classes: the B Special with a checkered stock of selected walnut, and the D Peerless and F Premier grades which featured progressively finer wood and more detailed engravings.

Obviously, DuPont management was in the firearms game to make money. It was estimated that the 721/722 rifles had to be sold at a 1500 per month clip in order to break even. When one considers the low production sales figures for pre-World War II rifles, a break-even point of 1500 specimens per month was indeed audacious—and the response of the market was overwhelming. People liked the rifles' light weight and good balance. Their speed and smoothness of operation was acclaimed. The clean stock lines and proportions, and the smooth-working, strong receiver were 'winners.' The safety was both noiseless and convenient, and the bolt handle and safety location were designed with low mounted scopes in mind. Even the trigger was adjustable—and best of all, the price was right.

Below: The Remington Model 788 is chambered for five calibers from .223 Remington to .308 Winchester, and has nine locking lugs. At right: The famous turn-of-the century sharpshooter Annie Oakley, the only woman to ever hold the 'World Champion Shotgun Shot' title, was married to trick shot Frank Butler, who became a Remington salesman. Annie's prowess was amazing, and she most often used Remington rifles and pistols. Here, however, she holds a shotgun which was custom-tailored for her in Great Britain.

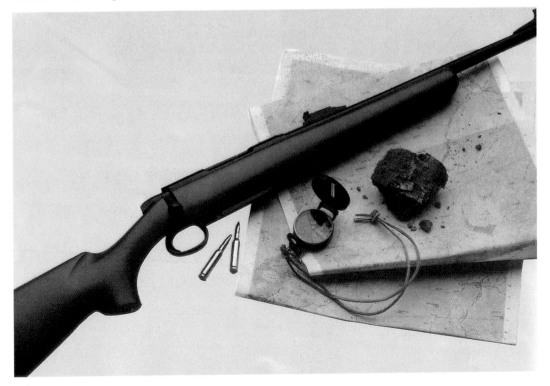

COPYRIGHT 1899
RICHARD K. FOX

The first year's production (1949) was approximately 46,000 rifles; sales in 1950 exceeded 50,000. Remington was selling everything it could ship. There was an early demand for checkering on the standard model stocks, but this would have boosted the rifle's base retail price by $10.00 to $15.00 and Remington opted not to checker the stocks. By 1951, sales had slipped slightly back into the 30,000 per year range, although coming years would see times when over 50,000 rifles annually were produced.

In 1962, the Remington model 700 was introduced, and it superseded the 721 and 722. Sales soared again, this time into the 60,000 per year category in the first year of production. Since that time, some years have seen over 100,000 of these rifles produced and sold. The Model 721/722 and their upgraded offspring, the Model 700, have set records as the best selling bolt action rifles in the world to this day.

One of the most interesting innovations generated by Remington Arms was that of the adjustable trigger. Up until the introduction of the Models 721 and 722, most rifle triggers were simply factory-set. But with the introduction of the new Remington rifles after World War II a new phase was coined in the every day usage of the firearms trade: 'The fully adjustable trigger.' This meant that the amount of effort required to pull the trigger in order to release the hammer could be adjusted according to taste. This is made possible via a secondary sear, located at the long end of the trigger lever, which allows the mainspring pressure to be drastically reduced. With only a small amount of pressure on this secondary sear, it is possible to maintain a small amount of contact with the mainspring. Small screws were mounted in the trigger housing which made it possible to adjust the limits of motion within the trigger mechanism—the weight of pull, creep, backlash and depth of sear engagement could be adjusted to suit sportsmen's finger reflexes. Naturally, Remington's competitors followed suit and virtually every deluxe new rifle which has been introduced since Remington's innovation has featured a fully adjustable trigger mechanism.

One objection that has been raised about the Remington Model 700 is that its extraction and ejection mechanism *looks* as if it's too small to be reliable—but looks can deceive. The extraction and ejection mechanism of a rifle is intended to clamp onto the spent shell and eject it from the breech when the bolt is pulled back. When one considers how a Remington Model 700 extractor works, apparent heftiness matters little. Remington extractors are somewhat unique: the more pressure is exerted on them, the tighter they hold onto the shell casing—this is the famous Remington 'ring of steel' bolt face extractor. The extractor derives its strength from the bolt itself and also cannot override the cartridge rim; when overriding takes place, the ejector gets 'stuck,' and fails to eject the spent cartridge. Remington put up with numerous complaints about their miniature extractors. Finally, their engineers concocted a tug of war test between a standard Model 98 Mauser extractor and the Model 700. The two rifle bolts were fitted into a laboratory setup which measured tensile

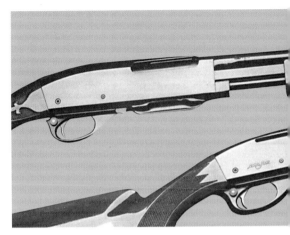

strength. The machine ran the pressure on each extractor up to hundreds and then thousands of pounds. The Mauser extractor let go first. The Remington extractor was triumphant.

As early as 1874, Remington was involved in the fabrication of beautifully made, single shot target rifles. The American team won an international competition over a crack Irish team that year at Creedmoor, Long Island: the Irish team was fresh off a victory at Wimbledon, England which declared them to be the finest marksmen in the Western World! Important in this victory were specially built 'Creedmoor' long range rifles made for the American team by E Remington and Sons under the supervision of L L Hepburn. Today, Remington's 40-X target rifle stands at the top of the accuracy heap. Many consider the 40-X to be the most accurate center fire rifle ever offered by a major arms manufacturer. Its accuracy is legendary and even rivals the efforts of the best custom gun shops. Today every 40-X that leaves the Remington factory is virtually a dream come true.

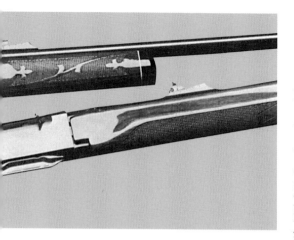

they are remarkable for mass-produced weapons.

Shotguns

Remington began producing double-barrel shot guns with the Remington-Whitmore Model of 1874, which was actually a shotgun and rifle combination. This particular 'do-anything' gun was produced from 1874 to 1882, when an actual double-barreled shotgun was produced in both 10 and 12 gauge. In the middle 1890s, Remington upgraded its shotgun technology by marketing a hammerless gun from 1894 until 1900. In 1907 Remington introduced its Model 10A Standard Grade repeating shotgun with slide action. This particular model proved to be quite popular, and continued to be sold into the late 1920s. About the time that the slide action shotgun was introduced, Remington came up with the Model 11A Five Shot Autoloader. This was a hammerless shotgun of the Browning type, with a tubular magazine holding four shells and available in 12, 16 and 20 gauge. Remington did not, however, confine itself to slide action and autoloader shotguns only.

In 1932, the Model 32A Over-and-Under Gun was introduced. This hammerless double-barrel featured automatic ejectors—and later models even incorporated a selective single trigger mechanism. It was available in 12 gauge only, but in various barrel lengths (from 26 to 32 inches) and chokes. Production ceased about 1942. In 1973, Remington introduced the Model 3200 Field Grade Over-and-Under Shotgun, which continues in production today.

But the accuracy game is not only played by bench rest shooters. Varmint rifles offer superb accuracy as well as conventional hunting features. One of the most accurate varmint rifles that can be had over the counter is the Remington 40-XB. This rifle comes in a variety of calibers from .22 up to .300 Magnum. The barrel is a heavy stainless steel tube. The 40-XB is available in both single shot and repeater models. Ultra-fine trigger pull is optional. Unlike other Remington firearms, 40-XB rifles are produced in Remington's custom shop and are hand built and tested. Each rifle is test fired for accuracy and the test targets are supplied with each rifle. The 40-XB stock profile and dimensions are beautiful to target and varmint shooters; the rifle is a stellar performer.

Remington also manufactures a very accurate varmint rifle known as the Model 700 Varmint Special, which is a variant of the Model 700 Sporter. Both the Model 700 Varmint Special and the 40-XB are direct descendents of the Model 722. The 700s are not custom built or fitted as are the 40-XBs, but

The Remington Model 870 is probably the most popular pump action shotgun of all time. In 1950, the first Model 870s appeared. These were five shot slide-action hammerless repeaters in various gauges, all of whose tubular magazines held four shells. Total sales are well over four million pieces. Pump action shotguns are generally used by those hunters who favor the reliability of manual operation especially in inclement weather and rough conditions. The 12 and 20 gauge 870s feature the interchangeable 'Rem Choke,' which is crafted from heat-treated seamless stainless steel and provides a wide variety of choke settings for the individual shotgun.

Today, the Model 870 Pump Action Shotgun comes in six varieties: the Wingmaster, the Special Field, the .410 Field, the Wingmaster Deer Gun, the 20 gauge Youth gun and the Express. There are also two special purpose 870s—namely, the SP Deer Gun and the SP Magnum.

Probably the largest selling *automatic* shotgun of all time is the Remington Model 1100 Automatic Field Gun, which was first introduced in 1963. This gas-operated autoloader is noted for its balance and soft recoil. It is marketed today in three basic varieties: the Magnum, the Field Grade and the Special Field. An array of separately sold barrels of various lengths, chokes and chambers make it possible for the Model 1100 owner to put his gun to its best

These pages, from the top down: **The Remington Model 7600 pump action; the Remington Model 4; the Model 40-XB-BR Benchrest rifle; the New Model 40-XB Kevlar Stock Varmint Special; the Model 40-XR Rimfire rifle; and the Remington Long-Range XR-100 Pistol.**

These pages, clockwise from far right: A ghost view of a Rem Choke choke tube as screwed into a Remington shotgun barrel; Rem Choke variable choke system tubes and their fitting tool; a ghost view of the mechanism of Remington's great new Model 11-87 Premier autoloading shotgun; and a closeup of the deep cut checkering on the 11-87's American Walnut stock.

Pressure Compensating Collar

Bolt Locking Lug
Powerful Extractor
3" Chamber (Except target guns)
Heat Treated Piston and Piston Seal
Stainless Steel Magazine Tube
Gas Port

use from upland game to flyaway shooting. The various Model 1100 versions are distinctively decorated with receiver scroll work, usually a high gloss finished stock, white spacers and the now-familiar diamond grip cap inlay.

The top-of-the-line Remington Autoloading Shotgun is presently the Model 11-87 Premier Autoloader, which utilizes a pressure compensating system which enables the shooter to use all loads—from heavy three inch Magnums to light 2.75 inch loads—interchangably. This particular gas system is completely self-cleaning. No matter how many rounds are shot, the compensating spring never has to be removed for maintenance. In lab tests, Remington has proven that its Model 11-87 is literally *twice as durable* as the most popular autoloader currently on the market. The 11-87 Premier features cut (not stamped) checkering and satin finish on an American Walnut stock. The Model 11-87 is also available in Special Purpose Deer Gun and Special Purpose Magnum models.

One of the newest innovations that Remington has introduced into the shotgun world is its SP MultiRange Duplex Shells. These shells are the first and only shotgun loads with a stratified payload; that is, heavier shot is loaded in front of lighter shot so that, when the shell is fired, the heavy shot breaks through any shot-deflecting brush and cover while the lighter shot retains its lethal energy for extended ranges. These multi-range shot shells are marketed in camouflage olive drab hulls with dull black bases. That this concept of two shot sizes in one shell is indisputibly effective is seen from a recent Remington test, in which new SP Duplex BBX4 shells were shot from 40 yards at a target moving 40 miles per hour. The resulting patterns showed 100 percent of the BB shot and 83 percent of the Number Four shot hit within a 30-inch circle. Most all of Remington's shotgun ammunition is available in both lead and steel shot.

Remington remains the only American ammunition company that also manufactures guns, and thus is able to tailor entire shooting systems to unique advantage, given the company's myriad ammunition product lines.

Below and bottom: This beautiful Remington Model 1100 autoloading trap gun—shown here in 'flip side' views—belongs to proud owner Mr Don Griffith, who has shot it with pleasure for many years. Another avid trap and skeet shooter is Air Force General Curtis LeMay *(at right).*

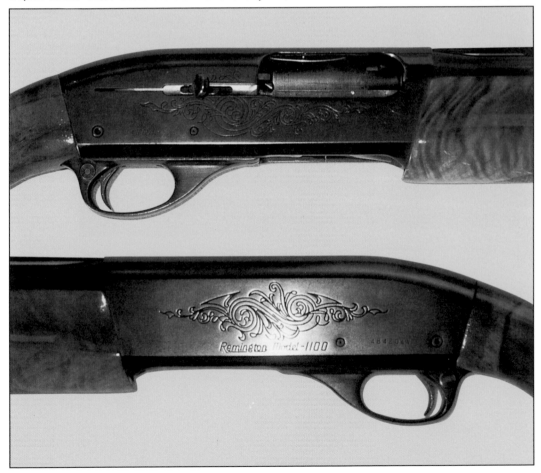

Remington Rifles 1816–1944

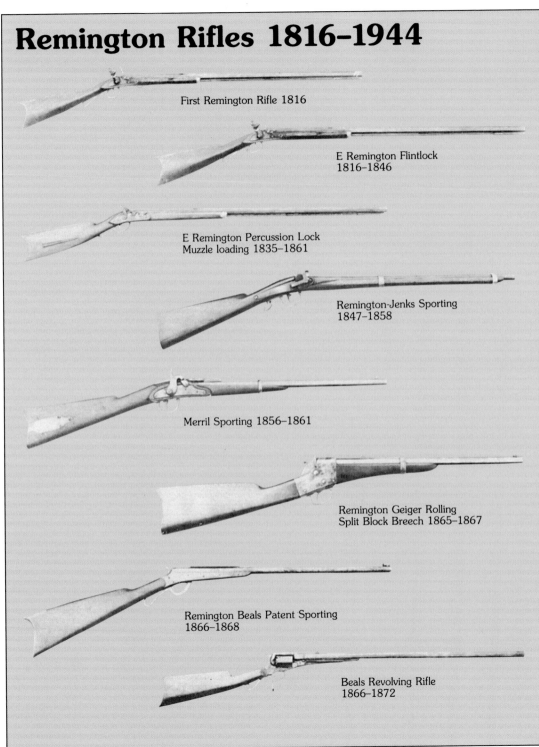

First Remington Rifle 1816

E Remington Flintlock
1816–1846

E Remington Percussion Lock
Muzzle loading 1835–1861

Remington-Jenks Sporting
1847–1858

Merril Sporting 1856–1861

Remington Geiger Rolling
Split Block Breech 1865–1867

Remington Beals Patent Sporting
1866–1868

Beals Revolving Rifle
1866–1872

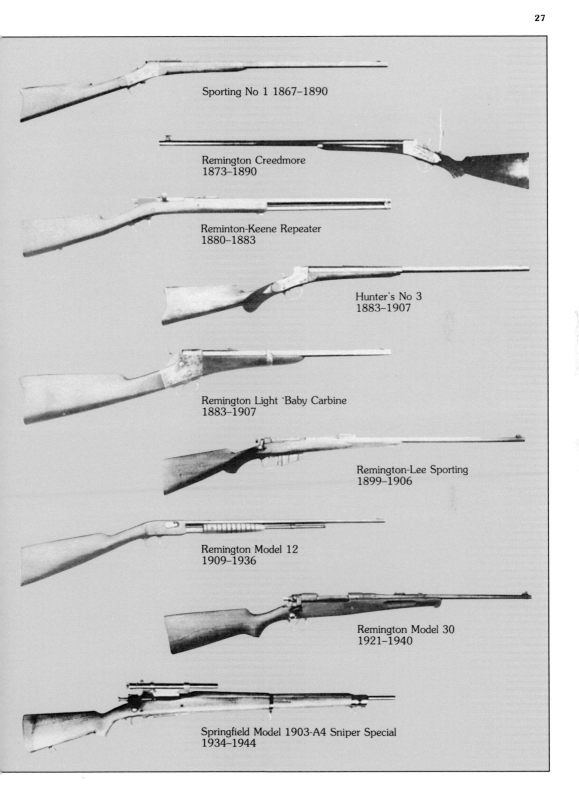

Sporting No 1 1867–1890

Remington Creedmore
1873–1890

Reminton-Keene Repeater
1880–1883

Hunter's No 3
1883–1907

Remington Light 'Baby Carbine
1883–1907

Remington-Lee Sporting
1899–1906

Remington Model 12
1909–1936

Remington Model 30
1921–1940

Springfield Model 1903-A4 Sniper Special
1934–1944

Remington Shotguns 1840–Present

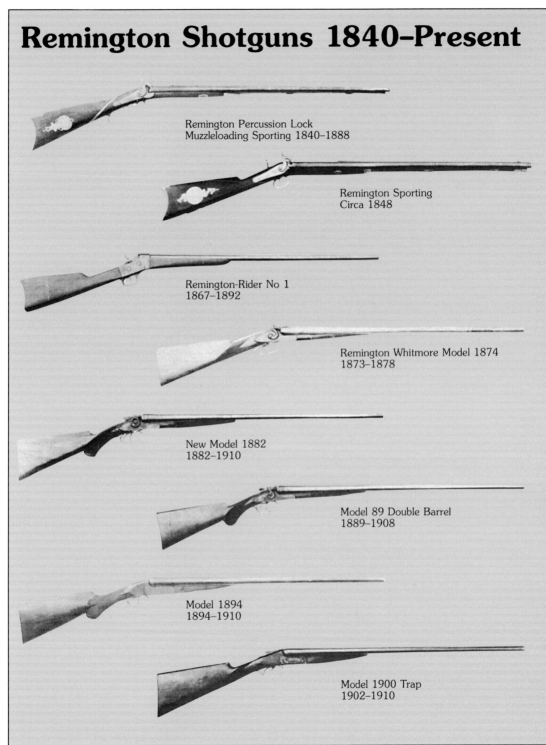

Remington Percussion Lock
Muzzleloading Sporting 1840–1888

Remington Sporting
Circa 1848

Remington-Rider No 1
1867–1892

Remington Whitmore Model 1874
1873–1878

New Model 1882
1882–1910

Model 89 Double Barrel
1889–1908

Model 1894
1894–1910

Model 1900 Trap
1902–1910

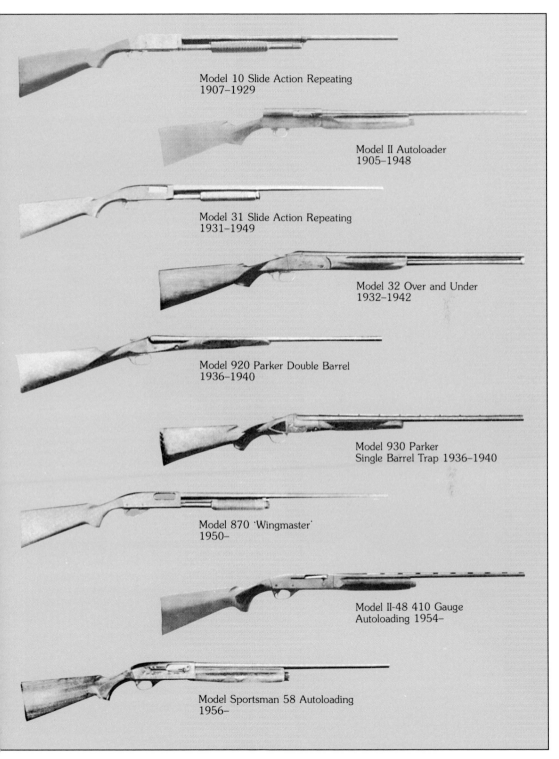

Model 10 Slide Action Repeating
1907–1929

Model II Autoloader
1905–1948

Model 31 Slide Action Repeating
1931–1949

Model 32 Over and Under
1932–1942

Model 920 Parker Double Barrel
1936–1940

Model 930 Parker
Single Barrel Trap 1936–1940

Model 870 'Wingmaster'
1950–

Model II-48 410 Gauge
Autoloading 1954–

Model Sportsman 58 Autoloading
1956–

Military

The same high quality that is evident in the sleek Model 7600 pump action rifle *(above)* has traditionally gone into Remington military arms. Remington arms have long had a central role in US history, as the display *at right, top to bottom* illustrates with one of 'Lite' Remington's flintlocks; a Remington-Jenks carbine; and developmental models of the legendary and far-famed Rolling Block rifle.

127 YEARS of SERVICE to the NATION

Arms

In 1845 the United States was preparing for war with Mexico. These preparations were hindered by circumstances in connection with the fact that the army was at that time equipped with muzzle-loading rifled muskets known as the 'Harpers Ferry Rifles.' These were to be produced by the John Griffiths Company of Cincinnati, Ohio, which held a contract from the government to produce 5000 units. The Griffiths Company was unable to fulfill its obligations on time; the government became understandably concerned, and let out the unofficial word to Eliphalet Remington that if he could see his way clear, the government would purchase rifles from him instead. Remington purchased the initial contracts from Griffiths and the government sweetened the deal by ordering an additional 5000 Harpers Ferry Rifles. Remington had to expand his facilities in order to meet this increased demand. He visited Chicopee Falls, Massachusetts and came in contact with the NP Ames Company. At this time, the Ames Company was turning out swords, bayonets and other military paraphernalia. Ames had also just contracted with the Navy for a new carbine invented by William Jenks. Remington bought the Ames Company, including all of its machinery, contracts and guns in various stages of production—as well as the services of his new-found friend, Mr Jenks. Jenks' original design was improved upon at many points. When finally delivered to the US Navy, the Remington-Jenks carbines were rifles with cast steel barrels, which were brightly tinned for protection against salt water, with hardened locks and breechs. The butt plate, trigger guard, sling rings, screws and other fittings were made of brass, polished to a high sheen. They were delivered to Commodore MC Perry's fleet in Vera Cruz in 1847, and were in the hands of his Marine troops when *they*

stormed into the fabled Halls of Montezuma.

With the introduction of the Remington-Jenks carbine, the US Armed Forces were finally out of the musket age. A joint Army and Navy board said of the Jenks carbine, 'The board is of the opinion that this carbine combines, in an eminent degree, the two great advantages attending arms loading at the breech—that of propelling the ball with great force and that of being loaded rapidly and easily in situations where the use of the rammer is inconvenient; the later consideration would recommend it for use in boat service and in the fighting tops of vessels as well as in the Cavalry service.' But startling new inventions, even when they carry with them overwhelming advantages, are not always recognized by the 'authorities' in power at the time. Lieutenant Colonel George Talcott of the Ordnance Department was resolutely opposed to the Remington-Jenks rifles. In a letter to the Secretary of War he said: 'A prejudice against all arms loading at the breech is prevalent among officers, and especially the dragoons. That the arms of Mr Jenks, even if found better than others, can be introduced is not to be supposed. As regards the arming of the Second Dragoons with them, Colonel Twiggs has protested in advance against the use by his regiment of any breech loading or patent arms of any kind whatever.

'There are now Colts, Jenks, Hubbels, Nuttings—and I know not how many other kinds of patent arms—that they will ultimately all pass into oblivion cannot be doubted. I am, sir, etc, G Talcott, Lieutenant Colonel of Ordnance.' As it happened, Talcott and Twiggs were the only ones to pass into 'oblivion.'

Before the US military accepted the Jenks carbine,

extraordinarily difficult requirements were imposed upon the Remington-Jenks carbines by the Ordnance Department. One of them was that the Jenks must fire 1500 times without any noticeable deterioration in its performance; the first such test went well until about the 1400th shot, when the nipple on the firing mechanism broke and the gun was subsequently turned down.

But Jenks knew that he had a good idea. He went to Europe and in England and France found governments that were more than willing to give him contracts. That the Europeans found the Jenks carbines very attractive caused the US government to awaken out of its close-minded slumber. In 1858, the Jenks carbine was redesigned to accept cardboard cartridges and was tested by the government once again. This time, the Ordnance Department tests consisted of firing the gun a mere 126 times. Then they loaded it, held it under water for a full minute, and set it aside. The next day the carbine was fired and, though rusted, no difficulty was encountered in putting 50 rounds through it.

By the latter 1850s, Remington was beginning to do an expanded business for other gunsmiths. In their catalogue for 1858, they stated that:

'We have acquired a practical knowledge of the gunmaking business, especially in the manufacture of barrels, which we believe few, if any others, possess, having during that time (40 years) tested a great variety of Iron for the purpose, but having mostly manufactured it ourselves expressly for our own use.

'We have also, for nearly 30 years, been testing the Steel of almost every manufacturer in the world, for our Cast Steel Barrels, and have for a long time had it made to our order expressly for that purpose.

'These repeated and long continued experiments, in procuring the proper material for every variety of Barrel, and an equally long experience in the various methods of working and annealing it, enable us to say, without boasting, that we are now prepared to make Barrels both of Iron and Steel in greater variety and perfection than any other Establishment in this country, if not in the world; having been first in successfully introducing Steel for Sporting Guns, and also for US

Rifles and Carbines, and having recently manufactured about 15,000 such for the US Service.'

Prices at this time ran as follows: cast steel barrels, $3.00 each; iron barrels, $2.00 each, Stubbs Twist (Damascus) $4.00 each; and matched barrels for double guns, (cast steel) $6.50 per pair.

The advent of the Civil War found the Union in dire straights. At that time, the government ran only two arsenals—one at Springfield, Massachusetts, and the other at Harpers Ferry, Virginia. But Virginia had seceded from the Union with the advent of war, and the Harpers Ferry arsenal was destroyed in the first days of the conflict. This left the Union with only one arsenal—which could only turn out a few thousand rifles a year. The government turned to Eliphalet Remington with the question, 'How many guns, revolvers and bayonets can you make for us?' The answer to that initial question was astounding. Orders from the Army and the Navy eventually amounted to over $29 million—a staggering sum in those days. At its peak, Remington produced over 200 pistols and nearly 1000 rifles per day for the Union troops. Dropforged bayonets were also produced by Remington during the war; 18,000 Maynard percussion locks were also built and used for the conversion of 1842-vintage flintlock military muskets. A cartridge division of the company was set up which supplied almost 10 million cartridges (which were primerless packets, each containing gunpowder, wadding and a rifle or pistol ball) to the government. Other deliveries included over 125,000 Remington-Beals .44 caliber Army revolvers, 5000 Remington-Beals .36 caliber Navy revolvers and 20,000 carbines. Of course, the bullet molds, reloading tools and other accessories for these firearms were also fabricated by Remington.

Such prodigious output of his factories naturally placed a severe strain on Eliphalet Remington himself. In August of 1861, his doctors diagnosed an inflammation of the bowels which today would be called an appendicitis attack. Overwork had simply caught up with him, and shortly before his death he dictated to his daughter, Maria, the following rather melancholy poem:

At immediate right: A Remington .44 caliber 'Old Army' cap and ball revolver of 1861. These well made and handsome pistols rode upon many a Union Army officer's hip. *Opposite page:* Often cited as the finest military rifle ever produced, the Remington Rolling Block was the first truly successful breech loading firearm, and reloaded swiftly; shown *at top and at middle* are flip side views of a Rolling Block saddle carbine. *At bottom, opposite* are all the metal parts required to assemble a Remington Rolling Block—all that's wanting are the stocks.

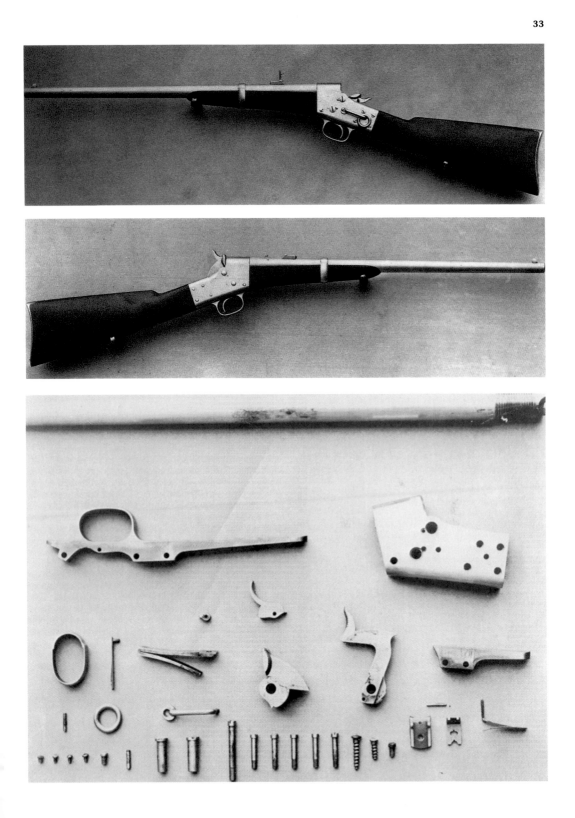

In manhood's strong and vigorous prime
I planted a young Linden tree
Near to my dwelling, which in time
Has spread its branches wide and free.

Oft I have viewed its healthful growth
With something like a parent's pride
Who sees the offspring of his youth
Grow to strong manhood by his side.

But now, old age has damped the flame
That glowed within me at that day
Energy and strength desert my frame
And I am sinking in decay.

But thanks! I've lived and long have shared
Health and vigor like this tree
And when I'm gone let it be spared—
A mute remembrance of me.

On 12 August 1861, Eliphalet Remington died. The business passed to Eliphalet's three sons, Philo, Samuel and Eliphalet, III. The sons continued in the footsteps of their father by importing promising inventors into the company. One such inventor was Leonard M Geiger, whose breech loading mechanism eventually became the basis for the famous Remington Rolling Block Rifle; however, the Geiger gun had a curious breech mechanism through which the hammer struck a rimfire cartridge. The Ordnance Department ordered 20,000 Geiger carbines, but since the Remington Armory was already awash with orders, these guns were manufactured by the Savage Company of Middleton, Connecticut under license from Remington. These guns were delivered in early 1865 and saw action in the last days of the Civil War. It is interesting to note that some of these Geiger carbines were equipped with small coffee grinding mills attached to the stocks; the Union army was not to be without its appropriate condiments around the campfire at night!

The Geiger carbines proved to be very successful against Confederate troops armed with ancient muzzle loaders. But because of the peculiar split-breech arrangement, certain weaknesses were noted in these carbines. An improved Geiger breech loader was presented to the board of the Springfield Arsenal in January of 1865. Competition tests were conducted including 65 other gunmakers—including Sharps, Roberts, Burnsides, Peabody and Henry—but it was shown that the Geiger gun needed further work.

Joseph Rider, in attempting to improve on Geiger's ideas, finally produced a gun that became known as the Remington Rolling Block Rifle. The Rolling Block breech was incredibly strong, easy to operate, and virtually foolproof. These single shot rifles have been praised as the best military arm ever produced. The breech was opened by simultaneously cocking the hammer and rolling the solid breech block straight back with the thumb. The backward motion of the block ejected the empty cartridge. A fresh round was shoved into the chamber, and the breech rolled forward and closed in one continuous motion. A locking lever secured the hammer while the gun was

open and locked the breech after it was closed. The firing pin ran through a hole in the solid breech block, with the hammer striking against the back of the pin, as it projected slightly from the block, at the moment of firing. Because of the unique nature of this rolling block system, the greater the recoil, the more securely the mechanism was interlocked; it was literally impossible to blow out a Rolling Block breech—which was capable of handling any ammunition then available.

Both military and sporting Rolling Blocks were produced. There were over a million of the military models and carbines made. The total production of the Rolling Blocks spanned a remarkably long period of gunmaking history, from 1867 until 1934. The Rolling Block was produced in four basic action sizes: the Number 1 Action was the largest of the Rolling Blocks and was chambered for the largest and heaviest calibers; the Number 2 Action was chambered generally for cartridges of medium-size and pistol calibers; the Number 3 Action was made in rimfire calibers of .22, .25-10 Stevens and .32; and the Number 4 Action was similar to the Number 1 in size and was designed for the 'smokeless high powered cartridges.' This last action was first introduced in 1898 especially for use with the then-new 'smokeless powder' cartridges, and was the last of the large frame Rolling Blocks.

The claim that the Rolling Block action was by far the strongest in the world was not lightly made. According to the report of Alphonse Polain, director of the proving house at Liege, Belgium, a .50 caliber Remington Rolling Block was loaded with 750 grains of powder (10 times the normal load), 40 balls and two wads. It was fired and the report states that 'nothing extraordinary occurred.' The Spanish government tested Remington Rolling Blocks by soaking them in sea water and then setting them aside to rust. When they were eventually fired, every metal part was coated with a thick film of corrosion but the mechanisms worked flawlessly. Various examining boards in different countries came up with incredible tests to which to subject the Rolling Blocks—the guns were fired over 2500 times continuously; stocks were removed and the guns were fired without them; metallic cartridges were filed down so that they would burst in the chamber; and ram rods were left in the barrels and shot out of them. Never a breech failed. Never a gun burst. All functioned perfectly. *Iron Age Magazine* of 7 March 1872 stated:

'The excellent shooting qualities of the barrels made at E Remington and Sons have been, from the era of the founder, a proverb in mouths of wisest censure. The superiority has been, moreover, quite as generally observed in the barrels of the military as of the sporting rifles. It is possible that a degree of this excellence may be due to the choiceness of material, but the extraordinary care given to the interior finish, the delicate gauging of the chambers, and the exact turning of the muzzles, and more than all, the patient and faithful straightening process, which is never neglected, are probably the general claimants in this instance... The Remingtons, with an honorable pride in the excellence of their production, and correctly estimating the superlative importance of this quality in a barrel, have omitted no care, whether it concerns the experience and skill of artisans, or the severity of intermediate and final inspection, that will secure the merit of precision for their work.' By 1872, the

Remington Armory was capable of turning out 1500 guns in a single day, all to exacting standards of quality. After the Civil War, the American arms market had slowed significantly. This was not the case, however, in most European capitals. European generals had studied the Civil War with meticulous care, and learned that muzzle loading arms were a thing of the past. But neither the Prussian Needle gun nor the French Chassepot—which were both breechloaders—could begin to compare with the new American single shot rifles. Opportunity knocked at Remington's door. The two other Remington brothers readily agreed that Sam was their best salesman. His personality was warm and charming. He was socially polished and witty. His *savoir vivre* would make him an instant hit in the extremely exclusive social circles of Europe, and could

win for the company many valuable contracts totalling millions of dollars. So that Sam could better deal with European royalty, he was elected president of E Remington and Sons in 1866. He sailed to Europe with his wife, Flora, and established headquarters in Paris, where he lived in opulent style. While upper class European society—and particularly, the royal houses—normally excluded tradesmen and industrialists from social events, the makers of firearms were welcomed with open arms. Sam was entertained in most of the royal palaces of Europe and his company's product, the Rolling Block rifle, was eagerly received by kings and military leaders alike.

However, not all of Sam Remington's endeavors met with success. Sometimes an excellent product backed by good salesmanship simply falls victim to sheer misfortune. The Prussian army had decided that the Remington Rolling Block rifles were the guns for them. Accordingly, Sam was invited to their maneuvers near Potsdam. Sam arrived on the scene resplendent in silk hat, Prince Albert coat, and riding a beautiful charger. The King of Prussia, soon to become Kaiser Wilhelm I, welcomed Sam graciously with the request that he would like to personally shoot Sam's rifle. Sam handed the piece to the king, confident of his majesty's approval. The king adjusted the sights, took careful aim at an oak tree about 100 meters away, and pulled the trigger. Nothing happened! A dud cartridge! Lady Luck had betrayed him! The king hurled the gun to the ground in a rage and galloped away leaving Sam Remington to muse upon the furies of Fate.

Remington's losing streak did not last long. At the Imperial Exposition of 1867 in Paris, the High Commission of Firearms unanimously selected the Remington Rolling Block Rifle as the best rifle in the world. The exposition's judges consisted of leading ordnance experts from France, England, Austria, Russia, Prussia, Spain, Italy, Sweden, Holland and Belgium. They awarded Sam Remington the Silver Medal, which was the highest award for both military and sporting firearms. Shortly after this, Ismael Pasha, the great Khedive of Egypt, sent a commission to France to inquire about the latest firearms with which to equip his new Egyptian Army. The Egyptian Commission called on Samuel Remington, who immediately set sail for Cairo to see Khedive Ismael Pasha. A close, personal friendship evolved between them. Khedive Ismael Pasha gave Sam an ancient scimitar of Damascene workmanship. What really impressed the Khedive was the fact that the guns specified in the contract actually arrived on the specified date—such efficiency was a rarity indeed, and must not go unrewarded! Sam Remington found himself owning a parcel of land in the most desirable residential district of Cairo. The only problem with such a gift was that when a parcel of land was given as a gift, the receiver was obligated to build on it or else be guilty of unforgivable discourtesy. Sam built an exquisite marble palace on this piece of property, but never

Below: Patent drawings for a US Army rifled musket. Remington made many similar arms for the Union during the Civil War. *Below right:* Patent drawings for the Remington Rolling Block rifle. *At right:* Late 19th century Remington arms displays, ready for shipping to firearms expositions around the world.

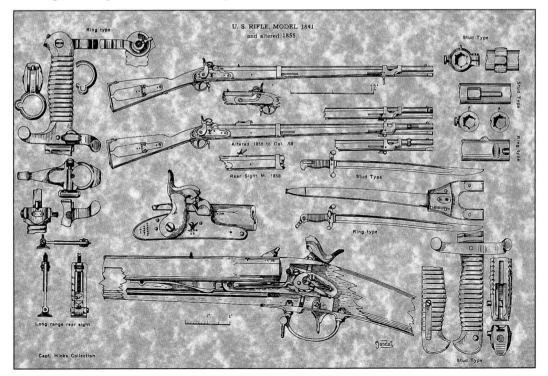

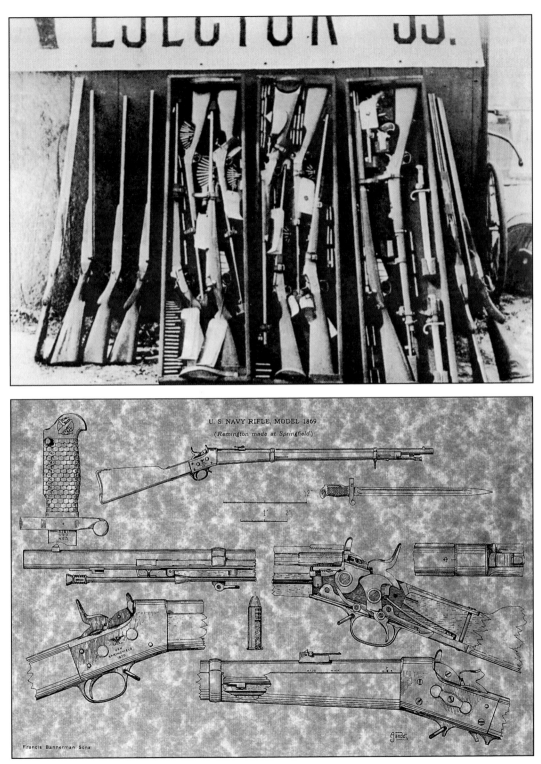

U. S. NAVY RIFLE, MODEL 1869

(Remington made at Springfield)

Francis Bannerman Sons

found opportunity to live in it. After his death it was sold to the British Government, who used it until 1952 to entertain VIPs in Cairo.

Historically speaking, one of the most interesting tributes to the virtues of the Remington Rolling Block rifles comes from none other than General George Armstrong Custer. In 1872, the General had purchased a beautiful Remington Sporting Rifle of the finest (F) grade for which he paid $91.50. Apparently he felt that he got his money's worth because he wrote to the Remingtons:

'Headquarters Fort Abraham Lincoln, DT
October 5, 1873

'Messrs Remington & Sons:
Dear Sirs—Last year I ordered from your firm a Sporting Rifle, caliber .50. I received the rifle a short time prior to the departure of the Yellowstone Expedition. The Expedition left Fort Rice the 20th of June, 1873, and returned to Fort Abraham Lincoln, September 21, 1873. During the period of three months I carried the rifle referred to on every occasion and the following list exhibits but a portion of the game killed by me: Antelope 41; buffalo four; elk four; blacktail deer four; American deer three; white wolf two; geese, prairie chickens and other feathered game in large numbers.

'The number of animals killed is not so remarkable as the distance at which the shots were executed. The average distance at which the 41 antelopes were killed was 250 yards by actual measurement. I rarely obtained a shot at an antelope under 150 yards, while the range extended from that distance up to 630 yards.

'With the expedition were professional hunters employed by the Government to obtain game for the troops. Many of the officers and men also were excellent shots, and participated extensively in hunting along the line of march. I was the only person who used one of your Rifles, which, as may properly be stated, there were pitted against it breech-loading rifles of almost every description, including many of the Springfield breechloaders altered to Sporting Rifles. With your Rifle I killed far more game than any other single party, professional or amateur, while the shots made with your rifle were at longer range and more difficult shots than were those made by any other rifles

in the command. I am more than ever impressed with the many superior qualities possessed by the system of arms manufactured by your firm, and I believe I am safe in asserting that to a great extent this opinion is largely shared by the members of the Yellowstone Expedition who had the opportunity to make practical tests of the question.'

I am truly yours,
GA Custer
Brevet Major General US Army

During the 1870s and 1880s, the best military weapons in the hands of world armies were still single shot affairs. It was seen that a great improvement could be made by devising a means of better facilitating the loading and ejection of cartridges from rifle breeches. Many mechanisms were invented to meet this end, but few were successful. At first, a magazine-type box was mounted on the side of the rifle, thus allowing the soldier to quickly find his ammunition supply. Later small springs were incorporated into these magazine boxes to allow the shells to be sprung upward as needed. It was not long before the idea caught on of mounting this spring-loaded box beneath the rifle and incorporating it somehow into the breech loading mechanism of the arm, thus creating a new type of repeating rifle. At first this sounded simple, but proved to be somewhat complex to achieve. Various masterpieces of mechanical complication were devised, none of which attracted the favor of military men. It remained for James Paris Lee, a Scottish-born American who worked for Remington, to do the job.

Lee's design was the ultimate in simplicity. The receiver was cut away underneath and a detachable sheet metal box was inserted through the bottom of it. The cartridges rested on an 'elevator' of sorts within this box, or 'magazine,' which was a loaded zig-zag spring. A spring catch held the magazine in place once it was pushed into the rifle. When the bolt was opened, the magazine spring moved a cartridge upward into the receiver. As the rifle bolt was closed, the cartridge was pushed forward into the chamber ready for firing. Soldiers could carry fully loaded magazines on their belts, and were availed of much faster reloading, and thus a greater rate of fire than ever before.

James P Lee was in fact one of the most brilliant of

Remington and the armament of the Indian Wars of the Old West. The lot of the US Cavalry soldier just got better and better weapons-wise; many were issued Remington Rolling Blocks, and eventually light armament evolved to include the bolt action, tubular magazine Remington/Keene rifle, such as is shown *immediately below*—which reloaded fast and held enough ammo in its magazine to preclude reloading with any frequency. The capacious tubular magazine which was located under the barrel of the Remington/Keene contained a long spring which pushed the ammo backward toward the breech, where, as a round was fired and its spent case ejected, another round was fed into the chamber for firing. However, most Indian scouts were supplied with single shot Springfield trap door models, such as those held by the Indians on the left, *at the bottom of the page, below*—in a scene from *Walk the Proud Land*, a Hollywood version of the American Indian Wars. Even famed fighting scouts such as Captain Taylor's squad, shown *at below right*, were issued the old Springfield carbines. Though Springfield was indeed the US Army's standard armorer, Remington was often called upon in times of war to produce such 'contract models' as these standard designs in enormous quantity.

Capt. Taylor and His
Noted Indian Scouts
on Drill at Pine Ridge S.D.
1891.
17.

all the inventors who had worked for the Remingtons. While still employed by the Winchester Arms Company, he had developed a refinement to the lever action repeater which replaced the Winchester Model 73. But he wanted to work at his own ideas for a bolt action magazine rifle, so he came to Philo Remington—who recognized talent, and gave him an entire workshop in the Armory and all of the technical assistance that he needed. Lee patented, on his own, the box magazine in 1879 and Remington began to manufacture the Remington/Lee rifle in 1880. Structural weaknesses in the breech resulted in several fatal shooting accidents, and these weaknesses were remedied. It is a testimony to the soundness of Lee's idea that the design was carried on, even with such early tragedy. Lee eventually perfected the design and

made it one of the safest guns in the world. Remington made the Remington/Lee rifle for the Lee Arms Company, which the inventor had organized as a selling agency. In 1884 Lee entered into an agreement with the Remingtons to both manufacture and sell his gun on a royalty basis. But by this time E Remington and Sons was in dire financial straits and eventually went into receivership, upon which Lee recovered the rights to his gun. Later, the British adopted the Lee system, in the form of the famous Lee/Enfield Rifle. This weapon was the standard arm of the British infantry for more than 50 years, even into World War II.

A curious legend surrounds James P Lee. In 1878–79, Lee lived in a room at the Osgood Hotel. He had a habit of bringing his drawings and models home at night, for further work. Remington also then employed a certain German mechanic by the name of Mauser. The story goes that Mauser bored a hole in the floor of his room—which was just above Lee's—and spend many hours flat on his stomach watching what went on below through the hole. The Mauser employed by the Remingtons was in fact the brother of Peter Paul and Wilhelm Mauser, the inventors of the Mauser Repeating Rifle: thus serious questions about the originality of the Mauser design persist. In any event, James P Lee is unquestionably credited with the invention of the box magazine and the Mauser Rifles were not so equipped until a number of years later.

The Spanish American War was a conflict that was short-lived, and thus had little effect on Remington and its partner, the Union Metallic Cartridge Company (UMC). The government did issue contracts, however, and Remington supplied rifles, while UMC made cartridges for the Army as well as brass cases for the six-inch shells with which Admiral Dewey's fleet won the battle of Manila Bay.

The summer of 1914 was one of unusual international tension. War clouds gathered upon the horizon of the world, but no one wanted to believe that war was possible. Archduke Francis Ferdinand, heir to the double Imperial Crown of Austria-Hungary, was shot by a Serbian at Sarejevo. Almost immediately Austria mobilized against Serbia. Russia mobilized against Austria in order to protect Serbia, in what Russia perceived as a religious war. Germany mobilized against France and France countered with its own defensive mobilization. The German armies surged forward and flowed over neutral Belgium. By the time the Germans were halted on the Marne, a short distance from Paris, the Allied governments had taken stock of their arsenals and found themselves in desperate need of guns and ammunition. Purchasing orders began inundating American firearms manufacturers in general, and Remington in particular. America was technically neutral, but its heart and hands were with the Allied cause. At first Remington produced a few thousand old fashioned Lebel rifles for France. Then the British ordered 1,000,000 Enfield

At left: Admiral Dewey on board the USS *Olympia*, at the Battle of Manila Bay—Remington made rifles, and the Union Metallic Cartridge Company made ammo for the US in the Spanish American War. *At right:* French troops of the 1880s, with Lebel rifles such as those Remington made for France some time later, in World War I.

rifles with the outlook that 1,000,000 more would be needed. Enfields had never been produced on a truly mass-production basis. It was up to the Remington engineers to retool their facilities to produce a maximum of 2000 guns per day. This meant that 3895 machines, 5905 fixtures, 7000 tools and 3415 gauges had to be revamped and/or fabricated, and mounted. Deliveries were to begin by 1 January 1916. This industrial miracle was actually accomplished a year ahead of schedule! Employment at the Ilion factory went from 1200 in 1914 to over 15,000 by 1917. Just before the United States entered the First World War, the factory turned out 61,000 Enfields for the British in one month!

The Imperial Russian Government was the last of the great Allies to come to Remington for help. But when they did, it was in true Tzarist style. The contract which was signed in 1915 called for one million Russian rifles and 100 million rounds of ammunition. The British contracts were already overwhelming the Ilion and Bridgeport factories. Whole new factories would need to be built in order to accommodate the Russians. In order to insure that his investment was protected the Tzar sent no fewer than 1500 inspectors to the Remington factories to verify that the 5000 Russian rifles that were coming off the assembly line every day met critical standards. The most irritating of these inspectors was a Cossack captain who became known as 'Alexander the Great.' His particular worry was that the rifles might fire accidentally. He would take a gun off of the assembly line, load and cock it and then bang the butt on the concrete floor with all his might. Of

course the rifles were too well made to accidentally discharge even when subjected to this kind of punishment, but as many as a dozen rifle stocks per day were cracked in this manner. Officials of the company could do nothing to stop this waste but the gunsmiths could. They filed down the locking mechanism on a particular rifle until the trigger literally hung by a hair of steel. They maneuvered this specimen into Alexander's hands. When the Cossack slammed the butt into the floor, the rifle naturally went off, and the projectile pierced a four inch pipe above Alexander's head sending a stream of water under high pressure into his upturned face, knocking him flat on his back!

By February 1917 the numerous Remington plants were producing at peak levels. Ilion was producing 2400 Enfields a day; the Bridgeport Rifle Factory, 5000 rifles and 5000 bayonets a day; and the Hoboken and Barnum Avenue plants, four million cartridges daily.

Then the unthinkable happened—all that had been Russia for almost 1000 years was overthrown! Tzar Nicholas II and his family were murdered. The Russian nation simply disintegrated into fragments, each fighting for its own survival. A provisional government under Alexander Kerensky was formed but lasted only a short time. Naturally, one of the first acts of the new Russian Republic was to repudiate all contracts that had been entered into by the Tzar's government. Remington had accepted the largest contract—and so was hardest hit. The Russian Revolution cost Remington millions of dollars in lost capital investment,

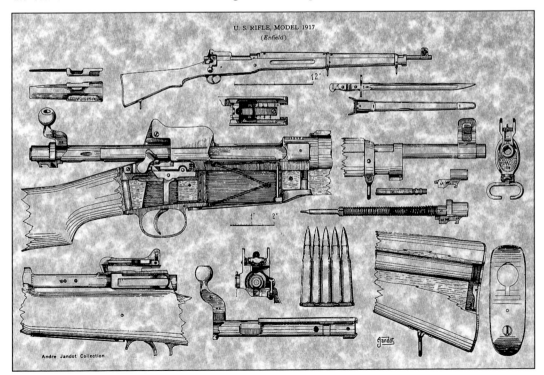

U. S. RIFLE, MODEL 1917
(Enfield)

12"

1" 2"

Andre Jandot Collection

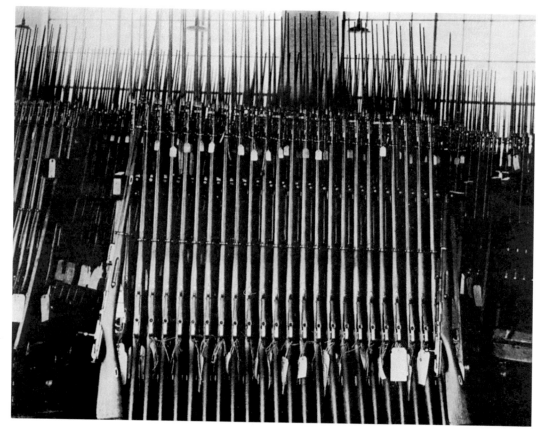

stockpiled hundreds of thousands of unwanted rifles in warehouses, and threw thousands of American workers out of work suddenly. But on 2 April 1917, America entered the War pledging its 'lives, fortunes and sacred honor' to victory. If the war was to be won, America had to arm four million troops in a matter of months. This was partially accomplished by government contracts to purchase 600,000 of the 750,000 Russian rifles already manufactured by Remington; this reduced the company's loss from an estimated $10 million to about $300,000. (It is interesting to note that some of these rifles were later shipped by the US Government to Vladivostok—on the eastern coast of what is now the Soviet Union—to arm the White Russian Army which attempted to rescue that country from the Bolshevicks.)

The Army Ordnance Department estimated that at least four million rifles would be needed within two years—at a time when there were approximately 700,000 Springfields in government arsenals, and the total manufacturing capability was 350,000 rifles a year; this left a net deficit of three million guns. Remington engineers suggested a radical solution to this problem. They proposed redesigning the British Enfield to take the Springfield .30-06 cartridge. This new US Enfield would be a far simpler gun to make and could be turned out in huge quantities by both Ilion

During World War I, Remington combined the British Lee/Enfield bolt action design (which was relatively simple for Remington to manufacture) with the new, powerful, Springfield .30-06 cartridge. The result was the potent Model 1917 *(opposite)*. *Above:* Some of the rifles Remington built for the Tzar of Russia. *Below:* US troops in France, in 1917: many carried Remington-made arms.

and other factories.

The new rifle was officially adopted by the Ordnance Department as US Rifle Model 1917. Remington retooled to make it, and other manufacturers also received large orders. By December 1917, production at Ilion was 3000 'M-17s' a day, and by June of that year production peaked at 4000 per day. Total production at Ilion was 545,541, while Remington's Eddystone plant produced 1,181,908 M-17s! By the war's end, over one million M-17s were stored in government arsenals. These were the same guns which would, 23 years later, be shipped to England after the British defeat at Dunkirk. These M-17s would play a pivotal role in saving Great Britain from a Nazi invasion.

Remington's production record for the World War I effort proved that a company whose foundation consisted of making sporting guns and ammunition could become one of the greatest industrial factors in the defense of the United States. Remington had produced 69 percent of all rifles manufactured for American troops during World War I and over 50 percent of all the small arms ammunition for the United States and her Allies. In addition, *all the ammunition* used by the Belgian Army in its four years of war was made by Remington.

In 1929, Remington sales amounted to over $21 million; by 1932, they had fallen below $8 million. At that figure, the company was losing money at the rate of nearly $1 million a year. Under these circumstances, merger or bankruptcy were the only alternatives left. Fortunately for Remington, EI DuPont de Nemours & Company of Delaware would come to the rescue. Some personnel at DuPont were skeptical about entering a new field—that of firearms production—because DuPont had up until this time had as its primary direction chemical operations and production. In the spring of 1933, the DuPont directors voted, but not unanimously, to acquire a controlling interest in Remington common stock.

The outbreak of war in 1939 had virtually no effect upon Remington's profitability. The strict neutrality laws of the United States made it impossible for US arms manufacturers to produce weapons for any country's war effort. But neutrality laws finally gave way to lend-lease agreements, which enabled US manufacturers to meet the growing British demands. British Prime Minister Winston Churchill sent his personal representative, Sir Walter Leighton, to Washington to get rifles from the US at any cost. England was in desperate need of several million improved Enfields, but the new British Enfield rifles were difficult to produce and no one was equipped with the machinery to do the job. If Britain wanted rifles in less than the two-year time span needed to tool up for production, some kind of compromise would have to be found.

The US government at this time had the machinery for making Springfield rifles at the Rock Island arsenal. If the government would lease this machinery to Remington, production of *Springfields* for the British could begin within a year—But the British wanted *Enfields*, not Springfields, and objected; they proposed that Remington retool the Rock Island arsenal machinery to produce the Enfields they wanted.

Remington's president took a strong stand against this proposal. US Army troops were equipped with Springfields, and if the machines were altered they could not produce spare parts if required. As events proved, this was indeed a wise decision. Final agreement with the British was reached in January 1941, and nine months later Springfield rifles began coming off the assembly line three months ahead of schedule. This was indeed a remarkable feat of engineering: the model 1903 Springfield contained 91 parts, whereas the new model A-3 contained only 79; 23 parts, previously requiring forging, were redesigned so that they could be stamped by presses—and only 24 parts remained unchanged. The bulk of these remodeled Springfields were not delivered to the British as America was thrust into the conflict herself on 7 December 1941; it was impossible to supply all of our men with Garands—then the standard US service rifle—so our 'Yanks' also got A-3s; the US Government took over the British supply contract, and Remington was now arming American troops. Had it not been for Remington President CK Davis' stand against retooling for Enfields, the GIs would not have had those guns when they needed them the most.

Remington's rifle production program was prodigious indeed, but did not compare with its production of ammunition. As early as June 1940, British contracts required the Remington Bridgeport facility to increase its production of .30 caliber ammunition by 600 percent and .50 caliber ammunition by 2000 percent! The capacity of the plant was increased with the understanding that at any time the capacity for further expansion would be used solely for the United States government, if needed. The British agreed to this provision and the job was begun. In the late summer of 1940, during the Battle of Britain, Remington was entrusted by the British government with a secret: bullets with an incendiary core. These were needed in .30 and .50 caliber. The incendiary bullet had to have exactly the same ballistic characteristics as both the ordinary lead core bullet, and the tracer bullet—otherwise they would be erratic in their flight. In less than a month, Remington had developed a working model of the bullet and had put it into large scale production. Later, the Army Ordnance Department would describe this accomplishment as, 'one of the vital factors in winning the Battle of Britain.'

In 1940, Remington had been approached by the Army Ordnance Department in Washington to prepare for war. At that time, in all of the Remington organization, there were only 360 men who had any experience with military ammunition. What the Ordnance people were asking for would require 40 times that workforce to be employed at Bridgeport alone. Remington management divided this almost

Opposite: A painting of the World War I Battle of Soissons. In evidence here are Remington-made Model 1917s, fixed with bayonets, in the hands of American 'doughboys.' *Above:* US paratroopers in North Africa prepare for action during World War II: note the Mooel 1917 leaning against the truck.

impossible task into two divisions; the company-owned factories, and government plants which had just been constructed for the exigencies of wartime production. Even though DuPont was overloaded with work, they let Remington take some of their best men—which eventually amounted to over 500 supervisory personnel.

Remington's Lake City Factory was the first modern facility to be designed for the express purpose of making military ammunition. Eventually it would consist of seven distinct manufacturing units—three for .30 caliber, two for .50 caliber, and one for .30 caliber carbine cartridges. Each unit was in fact a complete factory in itself. Raw material went in one end, and finished cartridges came out the other. This was the first time in history that ammunition was made in what was referred to as a closed cycle, meaning a continuous process. This was both a dangerous and difficult way of manufacturing; if through carelessness or mechanical difficulties a number of defective cases were to get into the works, the whole process of production would have to be stopped until they were cleared out. In actuality, this only happened once: the workers' deep sense of their great responsibility made for this extraordinary record of quality control.

It is interesting to note that during the whole of World War II, there was only one serious explosion at a Remington Plant; this occurred at a small storage warehouse at Bridgeport. The Navy had placed a hurried call for ammunition and the regular packing department, already swamped with orders, was strained to fill it. Men were set to work hurriedly nailing up cases and someone, it is thought, drove a nail into a primer. The explosion cost seven people their lives, and

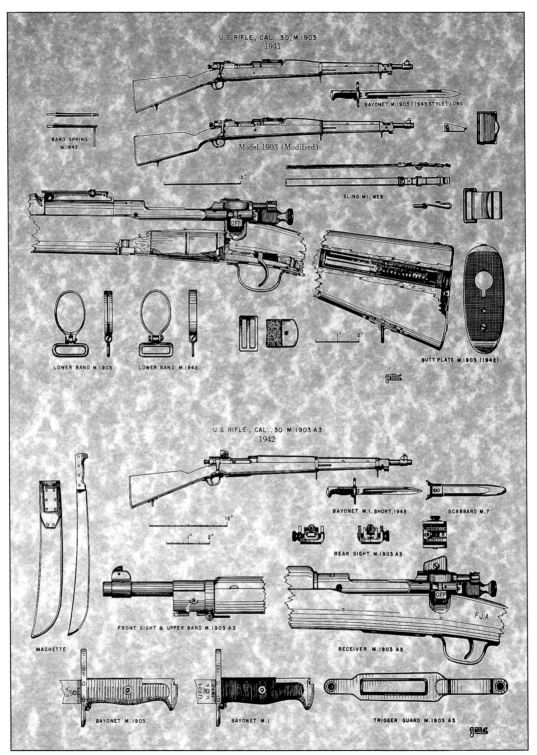

from that time forward, Remington absolutely refused to compromise safety on government orders no matter how urgent the request.

At its peak, the huge Lake City plant comprised 3800 acres, 25 miles of road, 236 major buildings, 11 miles of railroad track and parking space for 5000 automobiles. The plant had its own hospital, police and fire departments. Originally, the plant was designed to have a daily capacity of two million rounds of .30 caliber cartridges and 640,000 rounds of .50 caliber cartidges. This was stepped up to meet Ordnance Department requirements until, at the end, capacity was over 8.9 million cartridges per day.

But sheer production figures are not the only story. In 1943, over 14,000 people worked at the Remington plant on Barnum Avenue. This plant was unique among ammunition plants for the sheer variety of calibers and types of ammunition that were manufactured at one location. The list included ball, armor piercing, tracer and incendiary bullets; standard military cartridges; a wide variety of primers; shot shells and .22 caliber cartridges for training; and several types of cartridge for special purposes. These included such oddities as .45 caliber revolver cartridges full of birdshot (good for killing snakes) for downed airmen who had parachuted into South Pacific jungles, and 'frangible bullets' for soldiers in training to practice firing live ammunition at an airplane without endangering the pilot.

Remington at war. Above left: **Design drawings for the Model 1903 Springfield rifle, redesigned by Remington in World War II as the 1903 A3** *(below left). Below:* **Design drawings of the M1903 Springfield and M1917 Enfield—and the M1 Garand, which Remington did not manufacture.**

Remington licensed the US government and all designated manufacturers *without charge* for all Remington patents and technology—Remington even made its Research and Development Department available to the government. This R and D Department worked on a wide range of projects for both the government as well as private manufacturers. Among Remington R and D accomplishments are the development of a grenade launcher for the Garand rifle, super high-speed artillery projectiles, electrically fired primers for machine guns, a 12 gauge shell to start torpedo gyroscopes, new ballistic instruments and dozens of other devices.

It is clear from a historical perspective, why the government selected Remington to be its chosen instrument in building new cartridge plants. The Ordnance Department had established rigidly high standards of acceptance for military cartridges. These standards had been set up in peace time under the assumption that ammunition thus produced was to be done on a small production basis. When these standards were brought into gigantic mass-production operations, questions naturally arose as to their feasibility—but Remington had faith in its people, and set up standards even tougher than those of Ordnance. As a result, Remington not only met the 'impossible' government specifications—but in some instances actually raised them even *higher*.

Another historically significant fact about the huge expansions; vast training programs; the setting of new standards; the development of new types of ammunitions; the complex organizing of machine tool procurement; *and* the arrangements for obtaining the

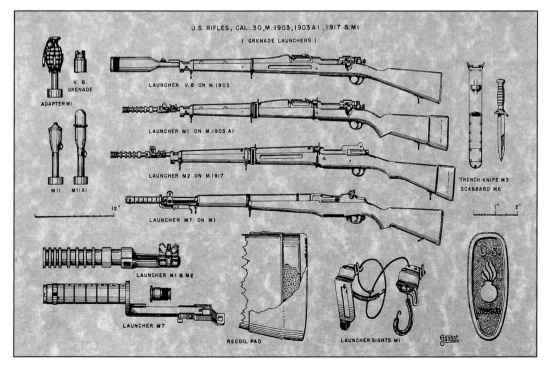

U.S. RIFLES, CAL. .30, M.1903, 1903A1, 1917 & M1

(GRENADE LAUNCHERS)

V. B. GRENADE

ADAPTER M1

LAUNCHER V.B ON M.1903

LAUNCHER M1 ON M.1903 A1

LAUNCHER M2 ON M.1917

M II   M II A1

12"

LAUNCHER M7 ON M1

TRENCH KNIFE M3

SCABBARD M6

1"   2"

LAUNCHER M1 & M2

LAUNCHER M7

RECOIL PAD

LAUNCHER SIGHTS M1

U.S.

huge stockpiles of raw materials was *planned* and actually *set into motion before* Pearl Harbor. The men who were in the know realized that war was coming, and their far sighted wisdom made for a United States military that was far more prepared for war than is generally supposed. Therefore, when war did arrive, it was only a matter of stepping up an already prodigious capacity for the production of small arms and ammunition. The output of the government's cannily-built new plants was doubled almost overnight. This was due to the streamlining of assembly line designs. For example, production in the units designated to make one million .30 caliber cartridges was raised to two million and units designated for maximum daily production of 640,000 .50 caliber were stepped up to one million. This was possible not simply out of luck, but was the result of far-sighted preparations. Hardly had the great new ammunition plants gone into full production before the US Army found itself practically snowed under by cartridges: as early as July 1942, Ordnance began shifting emphasis away from .30 caliber ammunition, and by the summer of 1943, at the very height of the war, cutbacks in production were ordered.

On 31 December 1943, five full months *before* D Day, the huge Salt Lake City, Utah, plant was ordered to cease operations and was placed in standby condition. Operations at the Denver plant ended on 31 July 1944, and the plant was converted to make fuses for artillery projectiles. All the requirements of the Ordnance Department had been met in 'overflowing' fashion. The government was justifiably lavish in its recognition of Remington's outstanding services during this critical period of American history. On 24 August 1942, the Army/Navy E—for 'Excellent'—pennant was awarded to the Lake City

plant. Both the Denver and Bridgeport Works were similarly awarded one month later. The Ilion plant received its award on 9 November 1942 and the Utah plant was honored in September of the following year. Remington's smallest plant at Findlay was given the right to hoist the Pennant of Excellence on 31 August 1944.

Many American corporations expanded fully 100 percent, and some grew up to 500 percent, to meet defense requirements during the war years. Few, if any, expanded over 2000 percent as did Remington: in 1939, there were fewer than 4000 people employed in all Remington plants; at the peak of production in 1943 Remington personnel numbered 82,500! (During this time over 15,000 Remington employees joined various branches of the Armed Services, and replacements were trained for them.)

Remington's safety record is nearly as astounding as its production records. In 1939 the major injury rate was 1.07 per million man hours worked. By 1942, the rate was only 0.88 and in 1943 it dropped to 0.67. Even though Remington plants were producing dangerous commodities, their safety record ranked far better than the average for general industry. Both the Lake City, Kansas and Denver, Colorado Ordnance plants achieved safety records which are among the best all-time performances in the history of industrial safety.

During the World War II years, Remington manufactured no fewer than 1,840,000 rifles and more than 16 *billion* cartridges for the US government. The ammunition statistic represents *41 percent* of all the small-arms ammunition used by the United States during that war for its own forces and for Lend-Lease.

Below: A sniper version of the Model 1903. *At right:* Remington handguns.

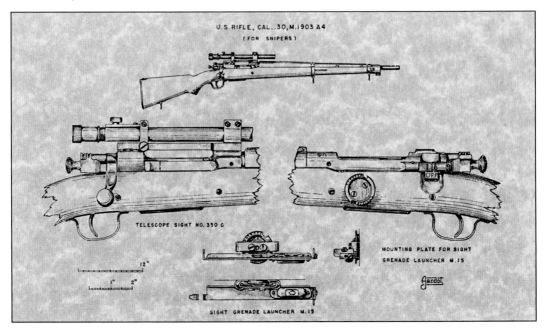

U.S. RIFLE, CAL..30, M.1903 A4
(FOR SNIPERS)

TELESCOPE SIGHT NO. 330 C

12"

1"   2"

MOUNTING PLATE FOR SIGHT
GRENADE LAUNCHER M.15

SIGHT GRENADE LAUNCHER M.15

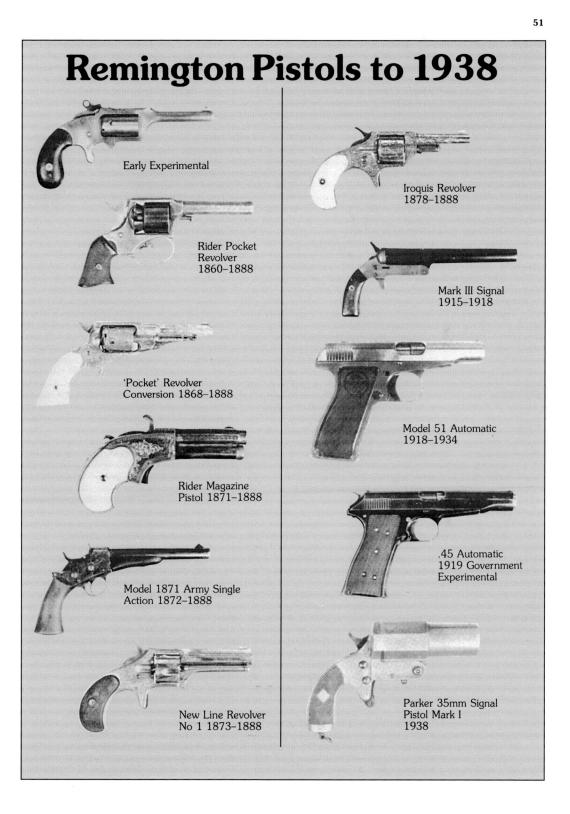

Remington Pistols to 1938

Early Experimental

Iroquis Revolver
1878–1888

Rider Pocket
Revolver
1860–1888

Mark III Signal
1915–1918

'Pocket' Revolver
Conversion 1868–1888

Model 51 Automatic
1918–1934

Rider Magazine
Pistol 1871–1888

.45 Automatic
1919 Government
Experimental

Model 1871 Army Single
Action 1872–1888

New Line Revolver
No 1 1873–1888

Parker 35mm Signal
Pistol Mark I
1938

Remington

The history of ammunition actually began in the 13th century, when Roger Bacon experimented with new ways of making what was then called 'Greek fire' by combining saltpeter, sulfur, and charcoal—and eventually blew himself out of this world in the process. Gun powder was thus invented—and not for another 600 years would the formula change appreciably. The first real advance in ammunition technology ocurred when a French gunsmith named Houiller came up with the idea of *encapsulating* projectile and powder, and thus made the first cartridges.

These early cartridges were made of various kinds of paper, cardboard or linen, and were easily broken or ruined by water. In the US Civil War, for example, wastage from such causes consumed 40 percent of the ammunition in the field. Some of these early cartridges had to be bitten open before loading so that the loose powder could spill out to be ignited by the percussion cap. Good teeth were thus a military necessity: for many years, the United States Army ran fresh recruits through severe dental tests to determine whether their teeth met evenly! (These standards were still in place until the middle of World War II when the Pentagon finally decided that no one needed to bite modern cartridges.)

In 1807, a Scottish clergyman named John Forsythe invented the percussion cap, which was simply a pinch of highly volatile fulminate of mercury sandwiched between two small copper disks which were shaped to fit securely over a 'nipple' in the breach of a firearm. When this 'cap' was struck by the hammer, the miniature explosion sent flame through the nipple into the powder charge in the gun's breech. The first half of the 19th century saw these ideas—the cartridge and the percussion cap—evolve into an idea about combining the percussion cap with the cartridge in one unit! German gunsmiths produced the 'needle gun' which was also the first bolt-action rifle: this weapon had, in place of the now-familiar firing pin, a long needle which penetrated the fulminate of mercury-charged base of a thin-walled cartridge, detonating its powder charge. The cartridges, however, were often unreliable and tended to stick in the chamber.

The first cartridge that was truly successful was made by the Maynard Rifle Company in 1851. It consisted of an elongated bullet set into a brass case containing the powder. The percussion cap was a separate affair mounted in the base of the shell. At this same time, Smith and Wesson produced an equally 'developmental' metallic revolver cartridge. The Volcanic Arms Company improvised on these ideas by making a hollow rim around the base of the cartridge and filling it with fulminate of mercury: this was the first practical rim fire cartridge.

With the invention of the metallic cartridge, the supremacy of breech loading guns was fully established. The fact that the brass cartridge would expand from the pressure of the explosion and thus automatically seal in all escaping gases and flames made these kinds of guns truly practical. The US Civil War was fought mainly with percussion cap firearms, but the conflict proved that these were obsolete. Any soldier, whether Blue or Grey, who had seen a Sharps or a Henry or a Remington Geiger wanted such a metallic

At right: A sampler of Remington ammo types, for all levels of sport. Remington has long been a major contributor to the advance of cartridge ammunition, and offers a full line of rifle, pistol and shotgun ammunition.

Ammunition

cartridge-firing breech loader.

Marcellus Hartley—perhaps the most brilliant of the arms entrepreneurs of the time—recognized that the trend toward metallic cartridges was fat with the possibility of enormous profits. Gunmakers usually had plenty to do in times of war, but in peace time, sport shooter and hunter would only buy two or perhaps three guns in his lifetime. However, Hartley reasoned that sportsmen would need to buy ammunition every year; thus the ammunition trade with its almost continual cash flow would prove to be a stabilizing influence in the otherwise 'boom and bust' firearms trade. Hartley and his partners bought two small New England cartridge companies—the Crittenden and Tribbals Manufacturing Company of South Coventry, Connecticut, and the CD Leet Company of Springfield, Massachusetts. Crittenden and Tribbals made the ammunition for the Spencer Rifle which Schulyer, Hartley and Graham sold. Hartley later moved the entire business to the Tribbals factory at South Coventry. Then he moved the whole operation to Bridgeport, Connecticut, and on 9 August 1867, incorporated and consolidated it all into the Union Metallic Cartridge Company.

The mechanical wizard AC Hobbs came to work for UMC and was soon put in sole charge of the manufacturing end of the business—a position which he held for over 20 years. During that time, Hobbs personally invented complete machinery complexes to move cartridges production beyond handwork and into all-machine operation. This automation not only vastly increased the speed at which ammunition could be produced and insured quality control but, more importantly, increased the safety factor of the operation as a whole.

One day a rather strange Armenian gentleman known only as Mr Azerian came calling at the UMC headquarters. After being taken on a courtesy tour of the Bridgeport operation, Mr Azerian identified himself as a representative of the Turkish Government and on the spot ordered 10 million rounds of ammunition. This was a staggering order for such a young company—and in time, some of the contract was signed out to the newly organized Winchester Arms Company. This one Turkish contract not only put UMC on its financial feet, but the surplus also assured the success of Winchester Arms.

About this time Colonel Hiram Berdan invented a new bullet configuration: it was accurate up to 300 yards. The Colonel also invented a breech loading mechanism known as the 'Berdan Slam Bang Breech.' This mechanism was used by the United States Army after the Civil War to convert muzzle-loading Springfields into breech loaders, and was also incorporated into the standard rifle of the Imperial Russian Army. Colonel Berdan's clever bullet was an ingenious modification of the then still-new rim fire cartridge. However, Berdan's cartridge had a percussion cap, or 'primer,' embedded in the center of the case surrounded by a flange of reinforcing brass: this 'primer' is known world-wide as the 'Berdan primer.' This was the first practical center fire cartridge and it was first manufactured by UMC at Bridgeport. The advantage of a center fire cartridge over rim fire ammunition was its enormously greater strength—due to the fact that you could make the casing thicker, since the firing pin had no need to dent the center fire case as it did the rimfire case. Much more powder and therefore more power and bullet velocity could now be packed into a metallic cartridge; the center fire was also more sure of firing and less apt to accidental discharge. The increased safety of the center fire cartridge is illustrated in the official report of the tests at the Frankfort Arsenal on 21 April 1868: 'A wooden box

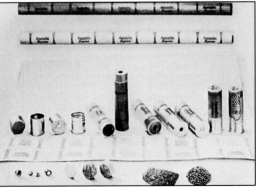

At left: The Union Metallic Cartridge Company, early on. *At top:* A 'shot tower,' in which molten metal falls from its pan *(at right)* into the shot-hardening tank. *Above:* Remington shotgun shell components.

Shotgun Shells

Immediately above: Remington's revolutionary Express Extra Range 'Duplex' shotgun shells feature two sizes of shot (*above right*, somewhat magnified) in the same cartridge—see 'Shotguns' in the Civilian Arms chapter, this text.

Below: An illustration of the performance of same. *Below right:* Remington's new nickel-coated buckshot on display, with cartridge and package of 10. *Opposite page, clockwise from bottom:* A selection of Remington shotgun shells; insertable chokes and wrench for the Rem Choke (see 'Shotguns') system; ghost view of a Remington Premier Target shot shell; sophisticated figure-eight wad from same; and Remington's advanced Premier 209 primers. Remington can coordinate the designs of its ammo and its arms, and thus fulfill any shooter's needs.

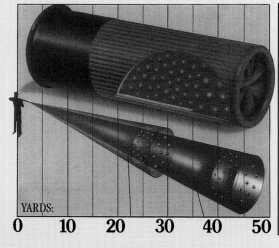

YARDS:

0   10   20   30   40   50

'Slugger'
Rifled

Buckshot

Premier

Nitro
Magnum

Express
Extra Range

ShurShot
Field Loads

ready for issue containing 680 metallic cartridges, caliber .50, in paper packages was fired into from the one-inch Gatling Gun. Three shots perforated the box and the upper layer of paper packages, destroying the upper half of the wooden box. The damage done was as follows; 29 cartridges exploded, 97 badly crushed out of shape, but not exploded, 38 loose uninjured, 480 in paper packages uninjured. The trial seemed to prove that the explosion of a caisson or an ammunition dump is robbed of its greatest terrors by being confined to only a small number of the few cartridges that may be struck by an enemy's shot.'

Due to Hobbs' inventive genius and to the terrific pace at which he worked, UMC got into large scale production only a few months after the contract with Berdan was consummated. These events would place UMC almost overnight in a commanding position in small-arms ammunition manufacturing. Unlike many inventions, the Berdan cartridge was an instantaneous success. The gunmakers of America as well as the rest of the world immediately began to adapt their locks to use the center fire principal. This was especially true of the Remingtons, who had just produced the famous

Remington Rolling Block Rifle. The combination of the new Remington breech loader and the UMC ammunition was simply unbeatable.

Hartley and his partners became the general sales agents for Remington, thus establishing the close cooperation between the companies which eventually resulted in their merger. The market for center fire ammunition was explosive. The Union Metallic Cartridge Company had one of the fastest growth rates ever recorded in American history. In 1867 it had only about 30 employees and one small factory; only four years later buildings had sprouted up all over the Bridgeport site and production was over 400,000 cartridges per day.

However, fast production and overwhelming quantities did not mean a sacrifice in quality. UMC ammunition was tested to very high standards, and these standards the company took pains to maintain on a rigidly consistent basis. For example, the bark *Forya*, bound from New York to the Russian fortress of Kronstadt with a cargo of 3,645,120 cartridges, was destroyed in a gale. Her deck was stove in, and the crew abandoned the water-logged hulk. Some days

later, the SS *Iowa* found the derelict barely afloat in a North Atlantic steamer lane. With salvage as their incentive, the officers and crew of the *Iowa* pumped out the *Forya* and towed her back to New York. The ammunition which had been under water for five weeks was taken out and shipped to Bridgeport. Tests were conducted and the report states, 'The wet paper boxes were removed and 10,450 of the cartridges were fired, proving them uninjured.' Twenty years later, more of this same lot were tested without a misfire. Another rigorous accidental test of UMC ammunition occurred in 1898; when the US battleship *Maine* was blown up in Havana Harbor, the UMC small arms ammunition aboard her went to the bottom. In 1911, her twisted hull was brought to the surface by Naval engineers and hundreds of these cartridges—which had lain at the bottom of a tropical sea for 13 years—were shot off without a single misfire.

Since UMC was not bound to any special type of arm, like the gunmaking companies were, it was free to make cartridges for everyone. The catalogue for 1872 listed over 30 separate patterns, including center fire, rimfire, cap and ball, and, generally, cartridges applicable to breech loaders of all descriptions—even the Gatling gun! By the early 1900s, the company was able to produce more than 15,000 different loads, varying from BB caps to 10 gauge shot shells. This tremendous variety was due to Hartley's determination that there should be a UMC cartridge for *every* type of gun that was made. This was not simple vanity for the benefit of advertising, but was the cornerstone of his business philosophy. That philosophy proved valid indeed.

With center fire cartridges squarely in the mainstream of the ammunition market, inventiveness lagged until the early 1920s. The fact that gun bores were subject to corrosive build-ups of residue after firing proved the need for general improvements in ammunition. Unless rifles were cleaned almost instantly after a day's shooting, or even after firing only a single shot, the shining bore would be coated with corrosion, and its polished perfection could possibly be ruined forever.

Below: **The interior of Marcellus Hartley and partners' firearms and munitions store. Hartley and cohorts formed the Union Metallic Cartridge Company.** *Opposite:* **Inside the UMC Bridgeport ammunition factory in the 1870s.**

Cartridges

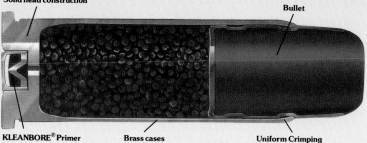

Solid head construction

Bullet

KLEANBORE® Primer　　**Brass cases**　　**Uniform Crimping**

Core-Lokt® Soft Point

Bronze Point™ Expanding

Power-Lokt® Hollow Point

Core-Lokt Pointed
Soft Point

Inside a modern Remington center fire cartridge *(above)*. *At left:* The tip of a Remington Soft Point bullet, a semi-jacketed projectile which features improved mushrooming upon impact for better knockdown power. *At right, from the top down:* A well-mushroomed Soft Point; cutaway views of various Remington bullet types. *Below:* The shiny brass and copper look of modern Remington center fire rifle cartridges. *Opposite, from left to right:* A selection of Remington rimfire ammo—.22 caliber blunt point antisnake bullets; standard .22 long rifle bullets; and .22 caliber hollow point bullets. Note that the first and the last of these are 'hyper velocity' rounds.

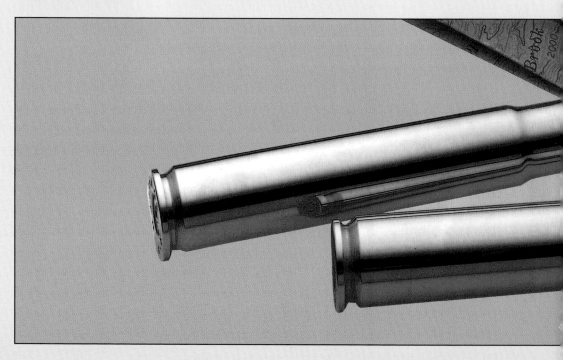

62

This damage was not caused by the erosion of the bullets or the smokeless powder, but by the chemical action of the fulminate of mercury and potassium chlorate used in the primers. Potassium chlorate was the real villain: it is akin to plain table salt, and absorbs water so quickly that even a minute grain would instantly begin a rusting process and eat a tiny hole in the steel.

In 1926 Remington introduced 'Kleanbore' ammunition which freed gunners from the incessant use of cleaning rags and powder solvents.

James E Burns, an imaginative chemist, paid a visit to Remington in the winter of 1924. He spoke of his plans for a trip to Florida, and then pulled out a revolver and began shooting—luckily with only primed empty cartridge cases. He requested that Remington technicians lay the pistol away in a damp place until he returned from his trip in about a month. When he returned, the revolver was examined: the bluing on the outside of the barrel showed streaks of rust—but when a dry rag was run through the barrel, the bore shown with pristine brilliance. Here was a chemical miracle! Burns had discovered a substituted for potassium chlorate in primers.

It took over two years of intensive experimentation before Remington was ready to go on the market with this new noncorrosive primer. The formula finally used contained lead styphnate, which was manufactured by DuPont. Extensive testing was carried out both in

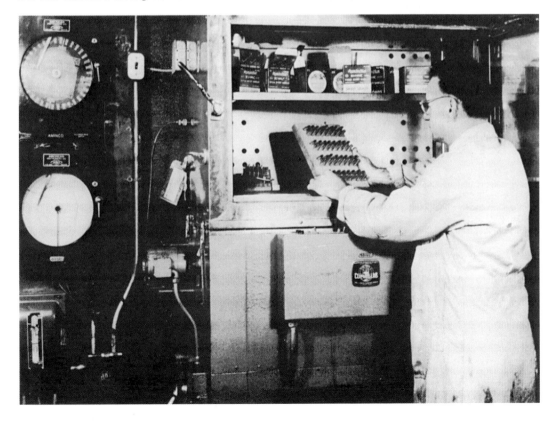

At left: Testing in the 1950s: A Remington technician places cartridges in a machine which simulates adverse conditions that exceed the most rugged of field conditions. *At right:* Another Remington technician tests new means of fabricating aluminum components for firearms during the postwar sporting arms boom of the 1940s and 50s; the war was over, and the hunt was on. *Above left:* A 1912 ad featuring the 'Remington Cubs.'

Remington's laboratories and also by special arrangement with various shooting galleries in New York state. Literally millions of rounds were fired in these tests. The guns in which the ammunition was fired were put through rigorous testing programs in which they were left uncleaned for 18 months after firing anywhere from 25 to 25,000 shots. Throughout the intervening years guns fired from 30,000 to over one million times without cleaning have still shown no signs of corrosion or erosion.

Other specimens were put into laboratory humidifiers which were run at 90 percent humidity at a temperature of 120 degrees. The outside of the barrels of these guns became encrusted with rust but in every case the bores came through in perfect condition. The new priming material formula not only failed to corrode, but actually *protected* the bores of guns through which it was fired. When the time came to actually market the noncorrosive ammunition, Remington held a contest to choose a name for it. Two men, separated by thousands of miles, had the same bright idea. WA Robbins of Jonesboro, Louisiana, and Nelson K Starr of Goshen, Indiana both suggested 'Kleanbore.' They each received a prize from Remington.

Remington introduced 'Kleanbore' ammunition to the general public in 1926, and though it is prudent to clean and oil one's firearm regularly, Kleanbore ammunition has helped to preserve many a gun bore. At present all cartridge companies make noncorrosive ammunition but, as in so many other firearm improvements, it was Remington that pioneered this revolutionary breakthrough.

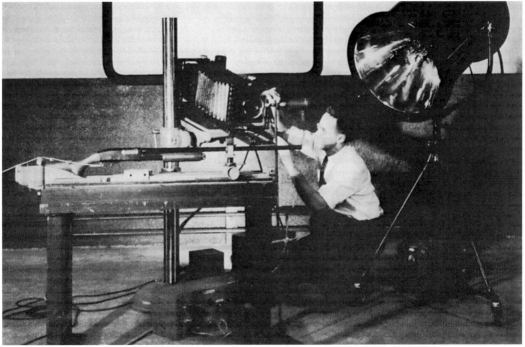

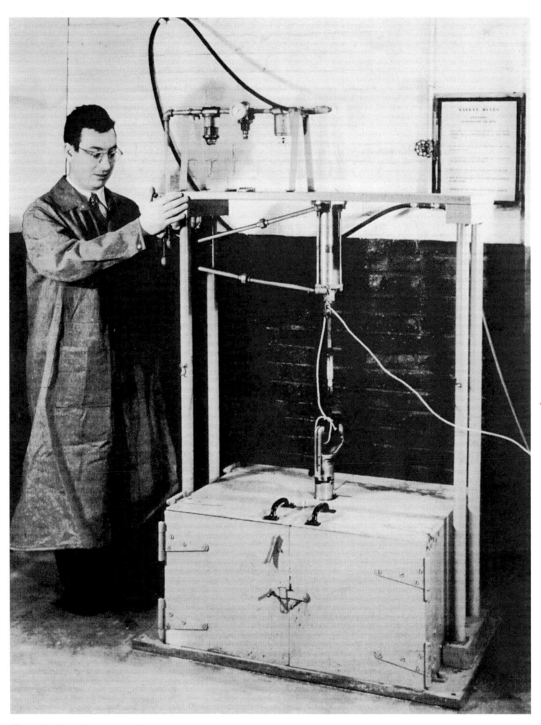

Above: Remington's experimental industrial tools, fasteners and cartridges have long been tested by remote control devices such as this. *Above left:* Features from Remington's famous Peters line of ammunition—the new 'Accelerator' bullets which increase muzzle velocity by almost 30 percent, and Peters .44 Remington Magnum semi-jacketed hollow point bullets. *At left:* Setting up a high-speed photo ballistics study.

Remington

It is a relatively little known historic fact that Remington, famous for its firearms and munitions inventions and innovations, was also the company to first perfect, finance, and market the typewriter. The first machine that would print faster than a man could write was invented by Christopher Latham Scholes who named it the 'Type-Writer.' Scholes was a printer and newspaper editor in Milwaukee, Wisconsin. He eventually sold the royalty rights of his great invention to his partner, James Densmore, for $12,000. Scholes is reported to have said, 'I have been trying all my life to escape being a millionaire, and I seem to have succeeded admirably.'

Scholes began his inventing process in 1867, and on 23 June 1868, he patented his first machine. During the inventive process, Scholes received helpful suggestions from young Tom Edison. Between 1868 and 1873, Scholes turned out no fewer than 25 different models, each improving on the last; the model of January 1873 was his final variation, and it actually looked like a modern typewriter, as it emobodied many of the basic principles of modern machines.

This model would only print capital letters, but it did incorporate the now-ubiquitous 'universal keyboard.' The arrangement of the alphabet was actually designed as a function of the desire to place letters that came close together in such a manner that they did not stick when struck in rapid succession. The acid test, of course, was whether a man could type as fast on a typewriter as he could on a telegraph instrument. This goal proved to be easily achieved, and Densmore and Scholes then knew that they had achieved a lasting place in history. Densmore immediately sat down at the new machine and—by way of reaching out for manufacturing capability and financial backing—wrote a letter to Philo Remington.

Remington, with some trepidation, finally agreed to meed Densmore and to look over the new contraption. Philo signed a tentative agreement with Densmore that same afternoon. This agreement developed into the contract that 'gave the typewriter to Remington.'

As it stood, the model of 1873 could not be produced on a large scale basis. William K Genne was given the assignment of perfecting the machine and redesigning it so that it could be produced profitably. Genne lost no time in this quest and the 'Remington Type-Writer Number 1' came out of the factory in September of that same year.

The Number 1 actually looked like a sewing machine. It was mounted on an iron stand with the familiar ironwork pattern on the pedestals and it even had a foot treadle which was hitched to the carriage return by a wire. The type arms were concealed in an ornamental iron case which had to be opened every time they stuck. The first catalogue typewriter ad describes the Number 1 as follows: 'The Type-Writer in size and appearance somewhat resembles the family sewing machine. It is graceful and ornamental—a beautiful piece of furniture for office, study or parlor.' The first year's production was a total of 18 machines and they were touted for their 'legibility, rapidity, ease, convenience and economy.' By 1878 the Remington Number 2 appeared; this printed capitals and lower case from the same keyboard.

But the public was simply not ready for such a leap into the future. Even though the public at this time was

Remington perfected and marketed the first typewriter from Christopher Latham Scholes' design. *At right:* A turn-of-the century ad for the Remington Standard typewriter. *Overleaf:* A Remington typewriter ad from 1920, by which time Remington Typewriters had been marketed for almost 50 years!

Typewriters

The World Asks More and More of Remington

Business is asking for more Remington Typewriters than our factories can produce.

That is the simple truth.

With the resumption of peace activities, European demand for the Remington rises rapidly to higher levels.

Remington's world-wide prestige was never so conclusively proved as it is this year.

This overwhelming Old-World preference is striking evidence of the high honor Remington has won during nearly a half century of modernizing the world's business.

It explains why, for forty-six years, the Remington has been known as America's business ambassador abroad.

In the New World, the appreciation of Remington advances equally with the demands across the seas.

Remington prestige at home keeps consistently ahead of Remington production.

Even with notable production activities, we are not able to give business all the Remington Typewriters it asks.

The past year was the greatest in the history of the Remington Typewriter business.

To make that record, the great Remington plants were taxed to the utmost.

And now, business at home, as well as abroad, finds need for more and more Remington machines.

Such preference can be based on only one thing—recognition, wherever typewriters are used, of Remington's incomparable contributions to the world's business development.

Self-Starting
Remington

Remington

Remington Complete Service At Your Call

For forty-six years, Remington has meant, to the business of the world, much more than the name of a typewriter. It has meant more than the name of America's oldest and best known typewriter manufacturer.

The world over, Remington typifies a service.

Today, both in number and in prestige, Remington stands first in continuous contribution to the modernizing and developing of the world's business methods.

To maintain the high standard of this world-wide business service, Remington has establishments in 586 cities.

Remington Sales and Service Cover the Civilized World

In every important center, in every country of every continent, Remington Typewriters and Remington Typewriter Supplies are leading factors in the conduct of business.

Remington Typewriters are made to write in 156 different languages. And Remington service goes hand in hand with Remington Typewriters.

Wherever Remington is writing the world's business correspondence, Remington typewriter papers, ribbons and carbon papers are also in demand.

It is estimated that the cost of the supplies used on the average typewriter exceeds the original price of the machine.

Without good supplies, good typewriting cannot be produced.

Remington service furnishes to all the world, therefore, typewriter supplies so superior that they win from business men, and from operators, the same generous praise which is accorded Remington machines.

Paragon Ribbons and Red Seal Carbon Papers

The same great business service that produced the Self-Starting Remington—which eliminates an average of 12 hand operations, and saves 48 seconds in typing each letter—also gave the world Paragon Typewriter Ribbons and Red Seal Carbon Papers.

Just as Remington Typewriters, for nearly a half century, have enjoyed unquestioned prestige, so also Paragon Ribbons and Red Seal Carbon Papers are world standards.

Remington is the recognized leader of the typewriter industry in the production of highest quality typewriter supplies.

In your own city there is probably a Remington office.

A call will bring you an expert—to show you how Remington machines will lower your typing costs, to give service on the Remingtons you are now using, or to prove the superior merits of Paragon Typewriter Ribbons and Red Seal Carbon Papers.

You have not reached the lowest level of office costs unless you use Remington Typewriters and Remington Typewriter Supplies.

REMINGTON TYPEWRITER COMPANY
Incorporated

374 Broadway   New York   *Branches Everywhere*

Remington Typewriter Company, Ltd., 144 Bay Street, Toronto

Key-Set Tabulating Remington

Typewriters

fascinated by such new inventions as the sewing machine, the electric light and the telephone, the Type-Writer was simply too expensive in terms of its use to the average consumer of the time: $125 seemed a lot of money to pay when you could buy a pen for a penny. Lengthy training was needed in order to operate the machine successfully and this also proved to be a barrier to successful marketing. Still another difficulty encountered was that many people simply did not like to receive personal letters that were 'machine written.' The Type-Writer was stepping on the intimate atmospherics of private communications!

One who *did* recognize the merits of the Type-Writer was Samuel Clemens. He apparently got the hang of his 'new-fangled writing machine' very quickly. In the first letter he wrote on it to his brother Orien, he said:

'The machine has several virtues. I believe it will print faster than I can write. One may lean back in his chair and work it. It piles an awful stack of words on one page. It don't muss things or scatter ink blots around. Of course it saves paper.'

Later Clemens would write to Remington:

Hartford, March 19, 1875
GENTLEMEN:
Please do not use my name in any way. Please do not even divulge the fact that I own a machine. I have entirely stopped using the Type-Writer, for the reason that I never could write a letter with it to anybody without receiving a request by return mail that I would not only describe the machine but state what progress I had made in the use of it etc, etc. I don't like to write

letters, and so I don't want people to know I own this curiosity breeding little joker.
Yours truly,
Sam'l L Clemens

The first typewritten manuscript ever delivered to a publisher bore these words upon its title sheet, typed on that Remington machine:

LIFE ON THE MISSISSIPPI
BY
MARK TWAIN

By 1886, E Remington and Sons was in serious financial trouble and was willing to dicker over its typewriter business with other manufacturers. The firm of Wyckoff, Seamens and Benedict would later that year purchase the Remington typewriter for $186,000. In time, the Type-Writer would be worth many, many millions of dollars.

Immediately below: Remington adding and subtracting typewriters were an advance in the 1920s. *Below left:* A Remington typewriter ad of 1900. *Below, bottom:* A 1926 celebration of the Remington Typewriter's 50 years in the trade. *At right:* Familiar designs are featured in this 1939 ad.

Remington Typewriter Company, Incorporated, New York City *(Branches Everywhere)*

For clear, clean, typewriter results, use Remtico brand letter paper, carbon paper and ribbons. Send for sample.

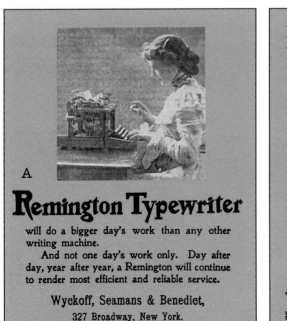

A

Remington Typewriter

will do a bigger day's work than any other writing machine.

And not one day's work only. Day after day, year after year, a Remington will continue to render most efficient and reliable service.

Wyckoff, Seamans & Benedict,

327 Broadway, New York.

THE SATURDAY EVENING POST

Remington – *The Official Typewriter of the Sesqui-Centennial Exposition*

Fifty Years of Progress

1876   1926

Remington
TYPEWRITERS

A MACHINE FOR
EVERY PURPOSE

Remington-made Paragon Ribbons and
Red Seal Carbon Papers always make good impressions

America's Typists are Swinging to Remington

OUR CHOICE!

THE NEW REMINGTON NOISELESS
Writing Perfection with Silence

In this, the 1939 model of the Remington Noiseless, more than ever are empha-
sized those factors which make for speed, comfort and convenience, in addition
to QUIET. Here is the one machine that will do everything demanded of a
typewriter not merely better, but *quietly*. In the general office, the private office,
the stenographic department, thinking and working are best done in an atmos-
phere of quiet ... and it is here that there is no substitute for the Remington
Noiseless.

For correspondence of the better sort, for matchless printwork, for manifolding
and stencil cutting par excellence ... for conserving and improving the nerves,
dispositions and abilities of the operator, executive and all within hearing, the
Remington Noiseless is supreme beyond all question. It is the world's finest
writing machine and one reason why America's typists are swinging to Remington.

With seven interchangeable carriages ... an exclusive Model 17 feature ... this one
typewriter, instead of several, will do all your wide form work. No other machine
can so quickly and easily be converted to take paper up to 31 inches wide. Here
is a very real saving both in capital investment and in floor space.

THE REMINGTON 17
The Completely New Typewriter

With this Model 17, the one and only typewriter that is *completely new*, Remington
steps into unquestioned leadership in the field of the so called "standard" machines.
In this classification, no other typewriter has so many wanted features, so many
exclusive improvements, so many obvious advantages. In no other typewriter will
you find the interchangeable carriage, that enables one Model 17 to do the work
of several wide carriage machines. In no other typewriter will you find such a smooth,
easy moving carriage, such a feather-light shift, a jam trip for preventing soiled
fingers and broken nails ... a so completely satisfying touch regulator ... in a word,
so many conveniences for the comfort and advantage of the user. This machine is
another reason why America's typists are swinging to Remington.

In the World of Tomorrow!!

CERTAINLY, A TRIAL WITHOUT OBLIGATION. CALL ANY REMINGTON RAND OFFICE TODAY

Remington Rand Inc.
BUFFALO • NEW YORK
Canadian Headquarters 970 Bay St. Toronto Canada

Remington Sewing Machines

Remington, as well as being, at times, in the firearms, ammunition and typewriter businesses, bought a little sewing machine manufactory called the Empire Sewing Machine Company, and thus entered the sewing machine trade. The firm of course became known as the Remington-Empire Sewing Machine Company, and eventually it was renamed as the Remington Sewing Machine Company. By the late nineteenth century it was to become familiarly known as such by many housewives, seamsters and seamstresses the world over.

At right is an early treadle model Remington, which was a similar type to the one that gave grandma lots of exercise as she mended, and sometimes made, grandpa's and papa's clothes. *At far right* is a flyer proclaiming the 'Remington Armory and Sewing Machine Works, Ilion, NY' in 1874. The pamphlet page shown *below* advertises Remington sewing machines in general, and dates from 1870–76. The page at *below right*, which is from the same era, specifies each model.

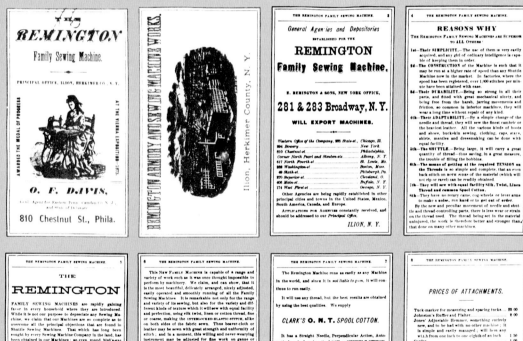

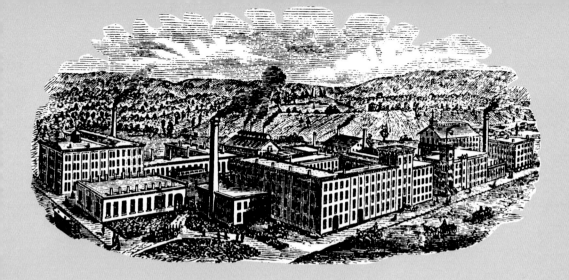

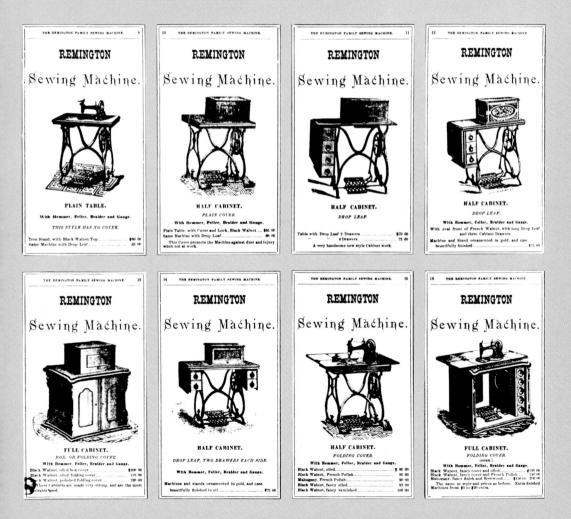

REMINGTON
Sewing Machine.

PLAIN TABLE.

With Hemmer, Feller, Braider and Gauge.

THIS STYLE HAS NO COVER.

Iron Stand, with Black Walnut Top......................$60 00
Same Machine with Drop Leaf................................ 65 00

REMINGTON
Sewing Machine.

HALF CABINET.

PLAIN COVER.

With Hemmer, Feller, Braider and Gauge.

Plain Table with Cover and Lock, Black Walnut.....$65 00
Same Machine with Drop Leaf............................ 68 00
This Cover protects the Machine against dust and injury when not at work.

REMINGTON
Sewing Machine.

HALF CABINET.

DROP LEAF.

Table with Drop Leaf 2 Drawers.......................$70 00
"   "   4 Drawers........................ 75 00
A very handsome new style Cabinet work.

REMINGTON
Sewing Machine.

HALF CABINET.

DROP LEAF.

With Hemmer, Feller, Braider and Gauge.

With oval front of French Walnut, with long Drop Leaf and three Cabinet Drawers.
Machine and Stand ornamented in gold, and case beautifully finished.................................$75 00

REMINGTON
Sewing Machine.

FULL CABINET.

BOX, OR FOLDING COVER.

With Hemmer, Feller, Braider and Gauge.

Black Walnut, oiled box cover.......................$100 00
Black Walnut, oiled folding cover.................... 110 00
Black Walnut, polished folding cover................ 120 00
These Cabinets are made very strong, and are the most desirable used.

REMINGTON
Sewing Machine.

HALF CABINET.

DROP LEAF, TWO DRAWERS EACH SIDE.

With Hemmer, Feller, Braider and Gauge.

Machines and stands ornamented in gold, and case beautifully finished in oil.............................$75 00

REMINGTON
Sewing Machine.

HALF CABINET.

FOLDING COVER.

With Hemmer, Feller, Braider and Gauge.

Black Walnut, oiled...................................$ 80 00
Black Walnut, French Polish........................... 85 00
Mahogany, French Polish............................... 90 00
Black Walnut, fancy oiled............................. 95 00
Black Walnut, fancy varnished........................ 100 00

REMINGTON
Sewing Machine.

FULL CABINET.

FOLDING COVER.

(OPEN.)

With Hemmer, Feller, Braider and Gauge.

Black Walnut, fancy cover and oiled.................$150 00
Black Walnut, fancy cover and French Polish......... 160 00
Mahogany, fancy finish and Rosewood......$150 to 200 00
The same in style and prices as before. Extra finished Machines from $5 to $20 extra.

Eliphalet First

Eliphalet Remington, II—'Lite' to his family and friends—lay asleep in a soft feather bed in the northeast bedroom of his father's house. Abigail, his young wife, lay beside him. The sun rose at 4:54 AM on that morning early in August 1816, and a first shaft of light, piercing the fringe of trees that rimmed the Remington fields, touched Lite's long, chiseled nose. He awoke, and remembering his plans for the day, heaved himself out of his feathered nest.

Abigail stirred and muttered, 'Is the night over already?'

'Yes,' said Lite. 'But don't you move. The women say you must be extra careful of the first child.'

'You're so good, Lite,' she answered. 'I'll keep him safe for you. Are you going to start the gun today?'

'Sure as shootin',' her husband said. 'The hay is in and things are slow at the forge. Father says I can use it.'

He put on a rough homespun shirt and pantaloons—broadcloth was for Sundays—pulled on his leather half boots, and went down to the hearty New England breakfast his mother had ready for him. He ate quickly, scarcely speaking to his parents, for in his mind he was already working the iron to form the barrel of his gun.

Legend says that young Remington asked his father for a gun; that he was refused on the grounds it was too costly, and that he went straight off and made one for himself. Legend often lies. In an era when game supplied most of the meat for every larder and the forest was still full of bears, wolves, and sleek, dangerous panthers, a gun was not a luxury but a necessity, and Lite Remington was not a man to go off without careful study and planning and make a gun by inspiration.

Remington, having carefully studied methods of gun-making, and having minutely examined all the rifles he could lay hands on, decided that he could make a better gun than he could buy, and he was quite right.

Lite finished his breakfast quickly, kissed his mother, and said to his father, 'Stop by the forge when you can and give me the benefit of your advice.'

'If you don't know more than I do about gun-making after all that studying, you'd better give it up right now,' his father answered. 'But I'll have a look at it all the same.'

Young Remington went out of the kitchen door, being careful not to bang it for Abigail's sake. He cut straight across the hay field in which the cows were now in pasture, toward the tall trees that rimmed the edge of 'the Gulph.' Ignoring the wagon track that quartered down its steep slopes to the ford near the sulphur springs, he slipped and slid down an almost vertical foot path between the great tree trunks that rose branchless for fully 60 feet before spreading out their thick canopy of leaves. The August heat was already on the fields, but in the wooded gorge the air was mostly chilly, and the steady rushing sound of the creek, rippling over its bed of boulders, made it seem cooler still.

The new stone building that housed the forge and smithy, which Lite's father, Eliphalet I, had built the year before, stood right on the water's edge. When it was operating, a wooden flume several hundred feet long carried water from a dam at the bend of the creek

Remington's Gun

Evidence of the oldest commercial firearms business in the United States. *Above:* This sleek Remington Model 600 in .243 Winchester caliber may serve to illustrate what a long way Remington firearms design has come since 'Lite' Remington first hammered out a barrel at he and his father's forge. But the flintlock that he made was no mean gun—its first public shooting trial caused many of the best shots in the land to buy barrels, parts and entire rifles that he, Eliphalet Remington II, had made. This was just the beginning of a way of thinking and a care of making that would enable the Remington Arms company to become, over the years, one of the greatest arms and ammunition makers in the entire world.

above the ford to the big waterwheel with its 12-foot wooden paddles. The water gate would remain shut today; the flume, empty; and the wheel still. Lite would not need them for the job at hand. Remington threw open the big door of the forge and left it so—it would be hot in there later. The interior of the shop was a scene of cluttered order. Nearest the doors was the wooden ox sling—stout, four-poster gallows on which oxen were hoisted to be shod since they could not give their feet to the smith as horses did. On racks along the walls hung dozens of horseshoes and even more of the little half shoes for the oxen's cloven hooves. Wagon wheels with shiny new iron tires leaned against the stone walls. In one corner were piled a heterogeneous assortment of parts for agricultural implements: harrow teeth and cultivator prongs, ox yokes, hoes, crowbars and the metal parts of other farmers' tools—including iron facings for wooden plows (it would be three years yet before Jethro Wood of Cayuga County invented the first all-metal plow).

In another heap were iron parts that the Remingtons made for the grist mills which were springing up on virtually every creek that could get up a sufficient head of water to turn a wheel. Mixed in with them were heavy sleigh shoes, curved to fit over the wooden runners of the only vehicle that could be used in that country from December to March.

In one corner of the shop stood the brick forge, its interior chimney already blackened with soot. Close beside it were the big circular tub bellows, a good six feet in diameter, mounted horizontally on a wooden frame. Within easy reach was the heavy triangular anvil, its iron column secured to a stout wooden block. The tools of the blacksmith's trade were racked handily by—sledge hammers, grooving hammers, wedge-shaped pritchel hammers for punching nail holes in the horseshoes, mandrels, rasps, paring knives, long-handled iron ladles for dishing out molten metal, chisels, gouges, files and powerful scissor tongs for handling the white-hot iron. At the south end of the building nearest to the waterwheel were big grindstones, laboriously cut from a red sandstone cliff in the Gulph.

Lite Remington hung a leather apron from his neck and went straight to the forge, where he started a fire of charcoal, which had been bought from the charcoal burners who worked their pits back in the hills—where the great trees provided an apparently inexhaustible supply of raw material. While the fire was getting started, Remington selected a rod of iron that he himself had smelted down from ore that had been mined in Frank's Fort Gulph, and from scrap iron which had been traded in by the farmers who were the Remington forge's best customers.

It took better than half an hour to get the fire exactly right. Then Lite shoved his bar of iron into the furnace and, swinging on the pole of the bellows, pumped it up and down, forcing jets of air into the coals which sparked and sizzled. The iron rod gradually heated to a cherry red that seemed brighter than the coals. Judging the right instant exactly from long experience, Lite seized the bar with the tongs and expertly swung it across the anvil. Holding it thus with his left hand, he raised a heavy hammer with his right.

Above: Eliphalet Remington II, aka 'Lite' Remington. *Above right:* The Remington homestead in Ilion, New York, where Lite was born, and in which he lived with his wife Abigail and his parents until the young couple moved into the house *(at right)* which Lite's dad built for them.

Stop here and take a look at him, for as the first blow rings upon the glowing metal, history will be made, and that small bar of iron will become the first of 10 million guns bearing the name of Remington. Lite had a long, loose-jointed body which in Sunday broadcloth seemed deceptively slender. Now, poised in tension for the blow, thighs and buttocks strained the rough cloth of his trousers, his bare arms were bunched with muscle and the rigid cords of his neck made a perfect pattern of human power.

So far he might have stood as the prototype of the young workman—the essence of physical strength and skill, single of purpose and beautifully adapted to that end. But the head poised on his straining neck seemed strangely out of context with his body: it was delicate, long and well-shaped with curly, dark hair growing to a widow's peak on the high forehead. Lips and nose were finely chiseled, eyebrows delicately sketched above large, dreamy eyes. Even in the flush of furnace heat and hard labor, sweat beading and dripping from the point of his classic nose, Lite Remington looked like a *poet*, which he was!

The hammer described a perfect arc and smashed down on the hot iron, sending up a spray of sparks. With the deceptive ease of practiced skill, Remington struck again and again in ringing rhythm. The end of the rod was beaten flat to a thickness of about one half

of an inch. When it cooled from red to pale pink, Remington swung it back to the bed of the furnace and pumped the bellows once more. Thus he worked it until the rod was changed to a long metal bar, one-half inch wide and one-half inch thick. Then he worked it over again until thickness and width were as nearly uniform as human skill could make them: this was only the first step.

The legend built around that gun has it completed in a single day, but it took a practiced gunsmith a week to make a gun, and must have taken Remington at least that long. After he had forged his length of iron, he took an arbor—the core around which he must build his barrel, for there were as yet no tools in the world that would drill a straight hole through three feet or more of metal—and fixed it in his vise.

Remington brought the strip of iron to red heat again, placed an end of it over the arbor and slowly bent the softened metal around the core so that it fitted in a closed spiral. Every few inches he would have to reheat it. It was close, arduous work, done with painstaking exactitude, for the tightness and evenness of the spiral, and the quality of the weld along its seams, determined the success of the whole undertaking.

While Lite worked, his father came by to offer approval and advice, and farmer customers dropped in to purchase goods and offer their opinions—since in the farm country of those times almost every man had at least a smattering of the blacksmith's craft, every man had his opinions!

The job was done at last. Lite Remington had produced a closed spiral of metal some forty-two inches long with a .4-inch arbor running through it. He laid this spiral in the bed of coals, and this time brought it to white heat. Then he sprinkled borax and sand on it to facilitate the welding process, and seizing it in his tongs pounded it vigorously on the stone floor. This was called 'jumping,' which was meant to jar the malleable edges of the spiral strip against each other so that heat-activated molecules would run together and weld the metal spiral into a solid tube of iron. Because only eight inches could be heated at once, Remington repeated this process six times—and there was the rough barrel of the gun!

Remington then plunged it, with a hiss and flash of steam, into a tub of water to cool. When he could touch it without burning his fingers, he drew out the arbor and eagerly raised the barrel, warm and dripping; he sighted along it to answer the vital question: Was it straight? As far as his eye could tell, it was. Then he looked through it, aiming at the open doors, and it seemed to him there was a slight divergence. To check this, he made a plumb line with a piece of string and a small weight, and dropped it down the tube. About a foot below the muzzle, the string almost touched the side of the barrel.

Marking the spot carefully, Remington rested the tube on two pieces of metal and taking a soft lead hammer tapped it smartly, several times. When he tried his plumb line again it was almost right. Two more slight taps, and now the line ran dead center down the length of the barrel, which was now actually 'as straight as a plumb line.'

E. REMINGTON & SONS

MANUFACTURERS OF
REVOLVERS, RIFLES,
MUSKETS & CARBINES,

For the United States service. Also,

POCKET AND BELT REVOLVERS,

Repeating Pistols, Rifle Canes, Revolving Rifles, Rifle and Shot Gun Barrels and Gun Materials, sold by gun dealers and the trade generally. In these days of house-breaking and robbery, every house, store, bank and office should have one of

REMINGTON'S REVOLVERS.

Parties desiring to avail themselves of the late improvements in Pistols, and superior workmanship and form, will find all combined in the New Remington Revolvers.

Circulars containing cuts and description of our Arms will be furnished upon application.

E. REMINGTON & SONS, Illion, N. Y.

MOORE & NICHOLS, Agents, No. 40
July 6—4m Courtland-st., New York.

For the last day's work on the barrel, Lite needed power. That morning he went first to the dam and hoisted the sluice gate. A fine head of water roared down the flume. Cascading over the end, it smashed down in flying spray on the 12-foot wheel, which shuddered and groaned and began to turn. Inside the forge the grindstones were revolving. Remington drove tapering wooden spindles into both ends of his barrel to act as handles, then pressed it vertically against the grindstone. The abrasive surface bit into the iron, sending forth a bright river of sparks. Lite gradually moved it against the wheel, cutting a flat, smooth surface the length of the barrel. Eight such surfaces were cut to give the barrel the octagon-shape that was then in fashion.

It took the better part of a day to grind the barrel. When it was done, Lite lifted it and caressed the polished metal, but the inside of the barrel was still rough, and he had no tools for reaming and rifling it.

The following day, Remington put on his best black broadcloth suit so that he would be properly attired for a visit to the metropolis of Utica. He slung a knapsack—packed with plenty of meat and bread—over his shoulder, clapped a tall beaver hat on his head, and carrying his barrel in one hand and his father's rifle in the other for protection against various carnivorous animals, set out for town.

Because it was much shorter and easier going than the River Road, he followed the old Oneida Trail along the crests of the hills. As soon as he left his father's fields, he plunged into the great woods; it was a little like diving into clear, cool water. The hot August sun was strained by the almost impenetrable ceiling of leaves to a dim green gloom, through which Lite saw an endless vista of dark, columned tree trunks rising to

Above: The old Remington family forge down in Ilion 'Gulph,' in which Lite Remington learned the blacksmithing business from his dad, Eliphalet Remington, Senior; they made farm implements and general smithing goods, including the occasional rifle barrel. When Lite made his first firearm, a flintlock rifle, response to the accuracy of the arm was overwhelming. Demand for Lite's barrels and complete rifles grew until Lite's dad had to build his son a company headquarters—and house (see caption, page 76). *Above left:* A Remington ad of 9 November 1866.

the high Gothic groining of branches and leaves. The white pole of an occasional birch was like a marker placed to show the way. Except for a thin spread of low ferns, there was no underbrush in that forest—the dense shade killed all vegetation that could not reach up to the light. The great trees stood a good 20 feet apart, so the only obstacles that Remington encountered were an occasional huge log fallen across the trail. Under his feet the forest floor, laid down through centuries by fallen trees and leaves and rotting vegetation, was delightfully springy to walk on.

Though the forest was so vast and dim, Lite did not feel lonely, for it was anything but silent. Indeed, it was as noisily conversational as a county-wide quilting bee. Away above him in the upper stories of the trees there was a tremendous traffic of birds. Crows, blackbirds and jays wrangled and disputed with hoarse croaks and shrill jabbering. Woodcock, plover and partridge talked to each other, and wild pigeons flocked in thousands, cooing low. Squirrels raced up and down the broad, bare tree trunks like flashes of gray light, and, on the ground, sudden scurryings indicated that minks, raccoons and other such valuable varmints were getting out of the way, while occasionally a deer flashed across the field of vision.

Remington noted the lively life around him, but he never broke his easy ground-covering stride, even while his imagination delighted in picturing the creatures who made all that commotion. But fanciful though he was, he probably never produced a mental image of his own angular person, top-hatted and in formal black, pacing through the aboriginal forest.

Except for a charcoal burner's aromatic pit and a thin trickle of humanity that he saw in the deep crack of Frank's Fort Gulph, he encountered no other signs of civilization until, after better than three hours walking, he struck the down slope to Utica. There the forest ended abruptly and he came out in the dazzling sunlight of open fields. Below him were the houses of

Above left: The Remington armory at Ilion, which was built in 1835. *At left:* Ilion, New York, as it was in 1883. The Remington Armory is at photo left. *Below left:* One of the canal barges which transported Remington products on the Erie Canal in the 1850s. *Above:* The Remington Arms plant at the corner of First and Morgan Streets in Ilion, New York, in the 1880s. *Below:* The Ilion plant at full capacity in spring of 1916.

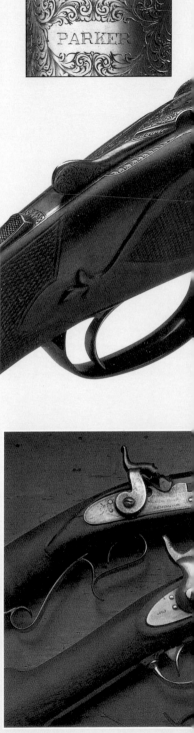

Above: An exemplification of the hand fitting and finishing which goes into every fine Remington firearm. The quality that is so evident in Remington arms throughout the company's history is the result of careful attention to detail—as is witnessed to by the astonishingly rich engraving on the Remington Parker double-barrel shotgun at *above right* (which view also evidences a closeup of the engraved 'Parker' appellation of same). *At above far right* is a portrait of Eliphalet 'Lite' Remington II, with family memorabilia; *at far right* is a very fine grade Remington double derringer from the 1860s amid familiar surroundings; and *at right, left to right,* handsome specimens of a Remington pre-Civil War cap and ball rifle with octagonal barrel, and a Remington cap and ball rifled musket of Civil War vintage with adjustable rear sight.

the fast-growing town, straggling from the hills to cluster thickly at the water's edge. He saw the brand-new mills and factories, fine church spires and the turmoil of commerce along the wharves. The Mohawk River's thin blue band, curving away between the hills, was speckled with activity. It was the one break in the great Appalachian mountain barrier from the Saint Lawrence to the Cumberland Gap, and through it funneled the mass migration of settlers, pouring out of the East to fill the vast vacuum of the fertile Western plains.

The river was crowded with long, high-sided bateaux and the big eight-oared Durham boats, with square sails set before the favoring wind. Oxen drew the new Pennsylvania wagons up the roads that ran along both banks, while other families moved westward on foot or on horseback, and occasionally in fine four-horse coaches.

Nor was all the traffic upriver. The fertile farms of the Mohawk Valley, the Genessee Valley and the Finger Lakes were the breadbasket of the Eastern seaboard. Their produce, and cargoes of salt from the famous salt springs of Syracuse, were floated down the Mohawk in strange lozenge-shaped vessels—half raft, half scow—that were called 'arks.'

Utica, with its population of 1200, was the biggest city Remington knew. As he walked down the steep hill of Genesee Street, it seemed very metropolitan to him and, in fact, it made up in bustle what it lacked in size. He inquired for the shop of Morgan James, a young man about his own age, who was making himself a reputation as a gunsmith.

Remington approached young Mr James with his barrel, and stated his need. James took it in his hands and hefted expertly. He peered along it and through it, and turned it over and over, inspecting the forging with particular care. Lite looked on with the agonized concentration of an artist exhibiting his latest work.

This was the first authoritative critique of his labors.

James soon put him out of his misery. 'That's a fine barrel,' he said. 'Straight as a string. It'll only take me a couple of hours to ream it for you, but the rifling is a long job.'

He secured it firmly in the narrow, wooden bed of his rifling machine, and introduced a nut auger mounted on the end of a slender five-foot rod. He turned the rod by a hand crank with infinite care, moving inch by inch into the barrel, cutting a smooth shining surface.

While the gunsmith worked, Remington never moved from the shop. He had no desire to explore the familiar sights of Utica. The grog shops and taverns by the wharves, crowded even at noon with teamsters and river men, were genuinely sickening to his fastidious mind. However, the new mills and the glass and cotton factories interested him intensely, for woven in with the poetic streak in his nature was a hard strand of practical ambition. The two elements of his character were twisted together like the steel and iron of an imported Damascus gun barrel to form the pattern of the man.

On previous visits to town, he had invariably visited its factories to examine new additions to their machinery and discuss economic problems with their owners. The rattle and bang of machinery, the crash of wooden spindles or the grating roar of slow-turning grindstones were a discordant symphony that drew him as strongly in one direction as the music of the forest did in another. It seemed to him a striking evidence of the fantastic prosperity of the times that experienced mill hands now made as much as 200 dollars a year. Where young workmen could do that, the sky was clearly the limit for an ambitious man with a little capital. Remington had every intention of jumping on the band wagon of industrial expansion, and he regarded the forge in the Gulph as a good base from which to leap.

At left: An early 20th century work photo of 'the Howards'— grandfather, father and son—representing 69 years of family craftsmanship at Remington. *Above:* The old Remington office building on East Main Street in Ilion, New York, which originally was Lite Remington's town house. *Below:* An 18th century photo of the Erie Canal at Ilion. See the canal barge photo on page 80. *Overleaf:* A Mohawk 600 with a Leopold 2x7 Vari-XII scope. The name Mohawk refers to the river which flows near Ilion, and the powerful Indian tribe for which it was named.

However, he had no time for factories this day; he wanted to study every move the master gunsmith made. So he ate his lunch in the shop, sharing a slab of ham and cheese and bread with James, while he cross-questioned the gunsmith about his craft.

When the reaming was done, they peered through the barrel in turn to admire its smooth sheen. Then James fastened it in the rifling machine again and, substituting a special cutting tool for the auger, began the infinitely delicate task of cutting spiral grooves inside the barrel. The bit cut a tiny fraction of an inch at a time, and James worked with an intensity that was matched only by his patience.

As soon as the light began to fade, the gunsmith knocked off. Remington spent the night with him and induced James—who loved his trade, and was to become famous at it—to talk about the history and technique of his craft. James began his tale at the beginning of America, and described the clumsy guns with which the Pilgrims had miraculously managed to supply themselves with game. Their matchlocks were so heavy that they usually required a forked stand to steady the barrel, and the charge was ignited by a slow-burning match like a piece of punk for lighting firecrackers. Then had come the wheel lock, in which a clockwork mechanism turned a steel wheel against a piece of flint throwing a stream of sparks into the priming pan. Finally, the familiar flintlock was invented by Dutch chicken thieves, who called it the *snaphance*, or hen snatcher!

All of these guns had been smooth bore and you were lucky to hit the broad end of a potato patch with one. However, German and Swiss immigrants, whose descendants are the Pennsylvania Dutch, brought the *rifle* to America. Their first rifles were German Jaegers weighing 20 pounds or more. They were unwieldy compared to the smooth-bore flintlocks then in general use, but with one you could actually hit a squirrel in the top of a tree. The trouble was that nobody could carry a Jaeger through the woods and besides that, it took special tools and about 10 minutes to reload, by which time the pioneer would likely be out of luck.

The immigrant German gunsmiths went to work on this problem. Through trading ideas among their many small, individual shops they gradually developed a long, graceful rifle that weighed less than 10 pounds and could be fired two or three times a minute. This was the 'Kentucky rifle'—it should have been called the 'Pennsylvania rifle.' It was perfected about 1730, and quickly became the most famous gun in the world.

'It was the rifle made the conquest of the Western wilderness possible,' James told Lite, 'but we Easterners (meaning New Yorkers in the parlance of the pre-Wild West days) were awfully slow about taking it up. We stuck to smooth bores until after the Revolution, and only now are rifles really becoming common hereabouts. It's still hard to get a good barrel. You've made a dandy.'

James finished the rifling job the next morning. When Remington paid him his fee—which was four double reales (two-bit pieces worth twenty-five cents each), still considered viable currency in the country districts—he felt that he had received more than his money's worth.

To complete his barrel, Remington had to bore a small touch hole near its base for the powder train, and had to forge a plug which he would screw into the rear end for the breech block. The firing mechanism was to be the then–universal flintlock. Remington forged the parts and finished them with a hammer, a cold chisel and a file. The lock consisted of a lock-plate to which he brazed a priming pan; a vertical strip of steel, which was held against the priming pan by a powerful spring; and a hammer, actuated by another spring, holding a piece of flint. When the trigger was pulled, the hammer slammed the flint down the face of the steel, uncovering the priming pan and throwing a stream of sparks into the priming powder from whence a flash of fire passed through the touch hole to the main charge.

In the evenings, Lite worked on the stock of the gun, shaping it from a straight-grained block of walnut with a draw knife, and whittling it out so that it fitted flush against the breech block, and exactly accepted the curves of the lock. He smoothed it down with a small block of sandstone—sandpaper had not been invented—and polished it with wild beeswax. The barrel was coated with hazel-brown, an excellent preservative made of uric acid and iron oxide.

On a Saturday evening, he assembled the gun, securing the stock and metal parts with hand-wrought screws and pins.

Not all the game in the world would have induced so strict a Methodist as Lite Remington to fire his gun off on Sunday. Besides, the sound of a shot breaking the Sabbath calm would have brought down on his head the ire of the Godly neighbors. But he would have been less than human had he not swung the new rifle to his shoulder 50 times that day.

He did not need the sun to wake him Monday morning. He took his gun, powder horn, newly molded bullets and greased patches to the field in back of the house. There he loaded with a heaping measure of black powder—might as well know if she'd take it—rammed the powder home and drove in the patch and bullet. He shook a pinch of powder into the priming pan and cocked the gun. Then he laid it on the ground with its butt against a tree, and tied a piece of string to the trigger. If she was going to blow up, he was too prudent to put his face in the way. He backed off, and knew a moment of irresolution while he thought of all the work that gun had cost him. Then he pulled the string.

There was a terrific explosion and the gun gave a convulsive leap spewing clouds of pungent black powder smoke. Lite ran through the choking fumes and picked up his gun: she wasn't hurt a bit.

Then came the real test. Lite reloaded with a normal charge and, aiming carefully at the bole of an ancient oak, pulled the trigger. The crash made his ears ring, and smoke blanked out everything in front of him. When it cleared, he saw the oak absolutely unscathed.

He fired again with the same lack of result, but on the third try, he got the hang of the thing. The bullet hole, centered beautifully in an irregular circle of bark, was the first of many Remington bull's eyes.

At right: Early cowboy movie star Tom Mix admires a fine custom shot-gun. Remington has long made excellent shotguns, with high-quality finish and meticulous care given to all aspects of each firearm.

How E
Entered the

It all began in the autumn of 1816, when Eliphalet entered a shooting match. Shooting matches were, at that time, the major sport of America. Tennis, golf and football were yet to be imported; it would be 20 years before the first baseball game was played at Cooperstown a couple of valleys to the south. True, the young men of the frontier had other amusements such as running races, wrestling matches and games of agility and luck, like trying to catch a greased pig. However, all these were minor accomplishments, good enough for a rough-and-tumble afternoon of fun, but were no great shakes compared to the more important art of sending a bullet as straight to the mark as the vagaries of handmade guns and highly variable black powder permitted.

Shooting for food and for survival was an essential element of life; but when shooting for sport, a man might display the skill of which he was most proud. These matches were held wherever a few men could get together in wilderness clearings on the outskirts of growing villages or towns. And the best shots competed on a county-wide basis—this counted as an organized sport in that part of the New World.

It was a county match that Remington entered. He had practiced all through August and September and was rather pleased with his marksmanship and his gun. On that fine October day, he found the crack

shots and their fans gathered in a clearing near Crane's Corners. Some wore the buckskin jackets of the frontier, others wore workaday homespun shirts and pantaloons and a few stood about somewhat self-consciously in black broadcloth and beaver hats. Lite was among the last.

There were in the crowd quite a few young women, who had come to watch the menfolk display their prowess. They wore long stout woolen dresses with sunbonnets or shawls on their heads, and they chattered together like squirrels, for it was not too often that they got together for a purely social occasion. The men, too, were in high spirits—boasting of terrific shots and improbable ranges, like bringing down a running buck at 150 yards.

When the shooting began, the horseplay ended—the women stopped talking as everyone tensely waited for the ear-splitting *whomp* of those long, big-caliber rifles and strained to see the result of each shot through heavy clouds of black powder smoke.

Remington seemed as calm as one of those expressionless wooden statues that amateur sculptors of the time liked to carve from tree trunks, but as he laid his gun in a forked rest and sighted along its brown barrel, his nerves were twitching. He was afraid he might make a fool of himself.

Remington Arms Trade

Above: Carrying the Remington tradition, this fine Remington 1100 SA Skeet autoloader comes in 12 or 20 gauge, and right or left-handed versions. *Below:* Tom Yule and Dale, the older of his two sons, adjust sights on their Mohawk 600 .222s.

That he did not do; nor did he win the match—but he placed second, which was not a small thing against the best shots in the Valley.

When it was over, the chronicles say that the county champion came over to congratulate Remington, and examine his gun. Then he asked leave to try it and shot better than he had in the match.

'Where did you get it?' was his question; and one can hear Lite answering with proper pride, 'Made it myself!' It seems that Remington had some difficulty convincing the men who crowded around that he was not boasting. When they saw he was serious, they were really interested. The champ was the first to ask what Lite would charge for a barrel.

Remington did a rapid mental calculation—so much iron, use of the forge, three days' work, a trip to Utica for reaming, a fair profit.

'I figure I could do it for 10 dollars,' he said.

'A fair price. When can I have it?'

Again Remington calculated. 'In about 10 days,' he said.

Other shooters wanted barrels or complete guns. Before Lite left the field, he was in the gun business.

At right: Montanan Tom Yule aims through his scope at a far target; Tom's Remington Mohawk 600 is a fine small game rifle, and in .222 caliber it has all the ballistic qualities needed. *Below:* The then-newly invented telephone inspired this 1899 ad for Peters smokeless powder cartridges. Though the dialogue is a bit unlikely, it gets the point across!

The Death
E Remington

Since building his first gun, young Remington had almost imperceptibly assumed the management of his family's foundry business. His father continued to run the agricultural manufacture and to do most of the building, but the rapidly expanding gun business was in Lite's hands, and the decisions concerning it were his. Soon, Lite's father took charge of building the little frame house on what is now Otsego Street, which was to be his son's temporary headquarters.

All the lumber for it was carted down from the Gulph in big drays pulled by four powerful horses each. Early on the morning of 22 June 1828, Eliphalet Remington I superintended the loading of a dray from the piles of 20-foot planks that were stacked in the drying yard near the sawmill. Then he mounted to the top of the high sweet-smelling load, while a young driver gathered up the reins. It was a hard pull up the hill, but the going was easier on the Cedarville Road. They passed the Remingtons' stone house, went down the hill into the Gulph again and crossed the wooden bridge with the dray's big, iron-tired wheels rumbling on the boards and the measured stamp of the horses' hooves like the rolling thunder of distant cannon.

Where the gorge cut between the crests of the hills its walls were several hundred feet high and a scant 200 feet apart. Here the untouched forest still stood in its somber splendor, and the bright morning was dimmed to a dusk so deep that the teamster halted to light his lanterns. Their yellow light gleamed dimly on the huge boles of the trees, and threw fantastic shadows as the dray moved on.

Beyond the heights, the road pitched sharply downward, and the horses braced themselves against the breeching straps to hold back the load while the driver leaned on the long lever of his brakes. Jolting and swaying, they moved slowly down the steep hill until, where the road made an abrupt curve to follow the course of the creek, they came to a sink hole. As one wheel dropped into it, the strain was all one way on the piled-up timbers. They slid a little between the holding stakes, and the whole load canted suddenly, pitching Remington off and ahead. There was no stopping the momentum of four horses and a heavily-loaded dray. The horrified driver tugged frantically at the reins and braked with all his might, but the equipage rolled inexorably forward, and a six-foot, iron-shod wheel passed over the dark body in the road.

Five days later Eliphalet Remington, father of Eliphalet Remington II—who was even then embarking on one of the greatest American enterprises in history—died in the fine stone house he had built in the wilderness. He died and his son went on, carrying the family name far beyond their little foundry.

Above right: **Tradition shines in an F-Grade Remington Custom Shop Model 1100 SA Skeet gun.** *At right:* **Part of the Remington Museum in Ilion, New York.** *Overleaf:* **Movie star Audie Murphy, and his sawed-off Remington Model 1882 shotgun in the 1960 movie** *Hell Bent for Leather.*

A Glossary of Remington Arms

Company Update

The close of World War II gave Remington the opportunity to retool its facilities to produce sporting arms. Large numbers of returning GIs were eager to pit themselves against less deadly foes than the war had provided. Hunting in America became a national passion with widespread popularity. North America was literally rediscovered as the habitat of many types of game suitable for sport hunting. Accordingly, Remington marketed numerous models of rifles and shotguns to suit the tastes and needs of everyone from the big game hunter to the field bird shooter. Bolt action rifles, target and sporting rifles, slide-action repeaters and autoloading guns were produced. Many advances were made in both the design of stocks and the ballistic characteristics of ammunition. It was a natural consequence, therefore, that Remington should involve itself heavily in various conservation movements. That same commitment is maintained today.

A glance at modern Remington product catalogues reveals that the company is presently marketing no fewer than three shotgun product lines, a half dozen or so rifle lines and a series of target rifles. All of this is in addition to both center fire and shot shell ammunition of almost countless types, sizes and specifications. However, a large product line has not meant that Remington has slackened its attention to detail. Their Custom Gun Shop caters to those who dream of owning a truly fine firearm. These custom guns are crafted one at a time to the dimensions, taste and style of the buyer. The F Grade Shotgun with Gold is one of two custom-grade shotguns available with personalized inlay and engravings. Various hunting rifles are also available from the custom shop, including the Grade Four Model 700 Rifle, the Model 40-XR Custom Sporter, the Model 700 Safari Grade Rifle, the Model 7 Custom with Kevlar Stock and the Model 700 Custom KS

Mountain Rifle. The Custom Shop even produces a handgun known as the New Custom XT-100 Heavy Barrel in .223 Remington.

Recently, Remington undertook to revamp its advertising, marketing and distributing techniques to better serve its many loyal customers. Remington prides itself in being committed to the quality of the hunting life. Their logo reads, very truthfully, 'Remington Country—It's a way of life since 1816.' That committment also produces a rare fact for a modern manufacturer in the world arena today: *Every* part of *every* Remington gun is not only designed, but built *and* tested in the USA.

Remington Handguns

Remington-Beals First Model Beals Pocket Revolver. Made circa1857–1858. Total quantity estimated between 4500 and 5000.

Percussion; .31 caliber. Five-shot round cylinder; three–inch octagon barrel.

Remington-Second Model Beals Pocket Revolver. Made circa 1858–1860. Total of about 1000.

Percussion; .31 caliber. Five-shot round cylinder; three–inch octagon barrel.

Remington-Third Model Beals Pocket Revolver. Made circa 1859–1860. Total quantity about 1000 to 1500.

Percussion; .31 caliber. Five-shot round cylinder; four–inch octagon barrel, spur type trigger.

At top of page: The Remington hunting arms logo—'Remington Country: It's a Way of Life.' *At right:* Tom Yule's sons Tim (left) and Dale (right) with a canine friend. Tim holds his .22 caliber single shot Model 514, and older brother Dale has his dependable Mohawk 600 .222 in hand.

These pages, from immediate right, counterclockwise: A Remington-Beals Army Model Revolver; a Remington Model 1865 Navy Rolling Block Pistol; a Remington Model 95 Double Derringer; a Remington Number 3 Revolver (which is often erroneously referred to as a 'New Line Number 3 Pistol'); and its design heir, a Remington Number 4 Revolver; a Model 1901 Target Rolling Block Pistol; and a Model 1890 Single Action Army Revolver.

Remington-Rider Pocket Model Revolver. Made circa 1860–1873; with altered specimens made for .32 rimfire metallic cartridge after 1873. Estimated quantity approximately 20,000.

Percussion; .31 caliber. Five-shot tapering cylinder; three–inch octagon barrel. Large, oval-shaped brass trigger guard.

Remington-Beals Army Model Revolver. Made circa 1860–1862. Quantity made estimated between 2000 and 3000.

Percussion; .44 caliber. Six-shot round cylinder; eight–inch octagon barrel.

Remington-Beals Navy Model Revolver. Made circa 1860–1862. Total quantity estimated at 15,000. Substantially identical in appearance to the Beals Army, but slightly smaller.

Percussion; .36 caliber. Six-shot round cylinder; 7.5–inch octagon barrel.

Remington-Rider Single Shot Derringer, aka 'Parlor Pistol.' Made circa 1860–1863. Total quantity less than 1000.

Remington Zig-Zag Derringer, aka 'Zig-Zag Pepperbox.' Made circa 1861–1862. Total less than 1000.

Caliber .22 short rimfire.

Remington Model 1861 Army Revolver, aka 'Old Model Army.' Made circa 1862. Total quantity estimated between 9000 and 12,000.

Percussion; .44 caliber. Six-shot round cylinder; eight–inch octagon barrel.

Remington New Model Army Revolver. Made circa 1863–1875. Total quantity estimated approximately 132,000.

Percussion; .44 caliber. Six-shot round cylinder; eight–inch octagon barrel.

Remington New Model (Single Action) Belt Revolver. Made circa 1863–1873 in percussion; made in cartridge model subsequent to 1873. Total quantity estimated from 2500 to 3000.

Percussion; .36 caliber. Six-shot round cylinder; 6.5–inch octagon barrel.

Remington-Rider Double Action New Model Belt Revolver. Made circa 1863–1873 in percussion with subsequent production as metallic cartridge model. Total quantity estimated at 5000.

Percussion; .36 caliber. Six-shot round cylinder; 6.5–inch octagon barrel.

Remington New Model Police Revolver. Made circa 1863–1873 in percussion with subsequent production as factory alterations to cartridge. Total quantity estimated at 18,000.

Percussion; .36 caliber. Five-shot round cylinder with safety notches on cylinder shoulder. Octagon barrel in 3.5–inch, 4.5–inch, 5.5–inch and 6.5–inch lengths.

Remington New Model Pocket Revolver. Made circa 1863–1873 in percussion; subsequent production as metallic cartridge conversions. Total quantity estimated at 25,000.

Percussion; .31 caliber. Five-shot round cylinder; safety notches on cylinder shoulders. Octagon barrel, available in three–inch, 3.5–inch, four–inch and 4.5–inch lengths.

Remington-Elliot Derringer 22 RF, aka 'Pepperbox.' Made circa 1863–1888. Total quantity combined for this .22 caliber with the larger .32 caliber model estimated at 25,000.

Caliber .22 rimfire.

Remington-Elliot Derringer 32 RF, aka 'Pepperbox.' Made circa 1863–1888. Total quantity of this and the .22 caliber type estimated at 25,000.

Caliber .32 rimfire.

Remington Vest Pocket Pistol, aka 'Saw Handle Derringer.' Made circa 1865–1888. Total quantity estimated at approximately 25,000.

Calibers .30, .32 and .41 rimfire.

Remington Model 1865 Navy Rolling Block Pistol. Made circa 1866–1870. Total produced originally estimated at approximately 1000; since revised to approximately 6500.

Caliber .50 rimfire; single shot; 8.5–inch round barrel.

Remington Double Derringer, aka 'model 95 Double Derringer,' aka 'Over-Under Derringer.' Made circa 1866–1935. Total quantity estimated at over 150,000.

Caliber .41 rimfire short; three–inch round, superposed barrels.

Remington-Elliot Single Shot Derringer. Made circa 1867–1888. Total quantity estimated at approximately 10,000.

Caliber .41 rimfire; 2.5–inch round barrel.

Remington Model 1867 Navy Rolling Block Pistol. Made circa early 1870s. Total quantity unknown.

Caliber .50 center fire.

Remington-Rider Magazine Pistol. Made circa 1871–1888. Total quantity estimated at approximately 10,000.

Caliber .32 extra short.

Remington Model 1871 Army Rolling Block Pistol. Made circa 1872–1888. Total quantity approximately 6000 plus.

Caliber .50 center fire. Single shot; eight–inch round barrel.

Remington Number 1 Revolver—New Model (Smoot's Patent). Probably most easily termed 'Remington-Smoot New Model Number 1, aka erroneously 'New Line Revolver Number 1.'

Remington Model 1875 Single Action Army Revolver. Made circa 1875–1889. Total quantity estimated approximately 25,000.

Caliber .44 Remington center fire.

Remington Iroquois Pocket Revolver. Made circa 1878–1888. Total quantity estimated approximately 10,000.

Caliber .22 rimfire. Seven-shot plain or fluted cylinder; 2.25–inch round barrel.

Remington Model 1890 Single Action Army Revolver. Made circa 1891–1894. Total quantity approximately 2000.

Caliber .44–40 center fire. Six-shot cylinder; 5.5–inch or 7.5–inch round barrel.

Remington Model 1891 Target Rolling Block pistol. Made circa 1892–1898. Total quantity shown on factory records at 116; however, larger quantities are possible.

Calibers .22 long and short rimfire; .25 Stevens; .32 S&W rimfire and center fire. Single shot; 10–inch half octagon/half round barrel.

Remington Model 1901 Target Rolling Block Pistol. Made circa 1901–1909. Total of 735 made, as indicated by factory records.

Calibers .22 short and long rifle rimfire; .25-10 rimfire; .44 S&W center fire. Single shot; 10–inch half octagon/half round barrel.

Remington Mark III Signal Pistol. Made circa 1915–1918. Total quantity approximately 24,500.

Ten gauge chambered for a special shot type shell charged with special powder only intended to fire flares. Single shot, nine–inch round iron barrel.

Remington Model 51 Automatic Pistol. Made circa 1918–1934. Total quantity approximately 65,000.

Caliber .32 (seven-shot) and .380 rimless (eight-shot). 3.5–inch round barrel.

Remington Model XP-100 Single Shot Pistol. Made circa 1963 to date. Bolt action.

Caliber .221 Remington Fire Ball; 10.5–inch barrel with ventilated rib; 16.75 inches overall. Weight 3.75 pounds.

Remington Rifles

Remington Model 1863 Percussion Contract Rifle, aka 'Zouave Rifle.' Made circa 1862–1865. Total quantity 12,501. Caliber .58; single shot muzzle loader; 33–inch round barrel.

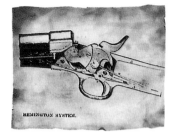

REMINGTON SYSTEM.

Remington Single Shot Breech-Loading Carbine, aka 'Split Breech Remington.' Made circa 1864–1866.
Calibers .46 and .50 rimfire. The predecessor of the famed 'Rolling Block' design; 20–inch round barrel.

Remington-Beals Single Shot Rifle. Made circa 1866–1868. Quantity unknown; estimated at less than 800.

Remington Revolving Percussion Rifle. Made circa 1866–1879. Total quantity estimated at less than 1000.
Calibers .36 and .44; six-shot round cylinder.

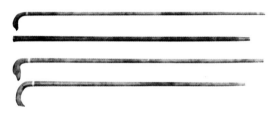

Rifle Cane, aka 'Cane Gun.' Made circa 1858–1866 in percussion; made 1866 to circa 1888 in breech-loading metallic cartridge model. Total quantity estimated at 4500.
Cartridge models made in .22 rimfire and .32 rimfire. Barrel length approximately 26 inches.

Remington Rolling Block Military Rifles and Carbines. Large Number 1 size action. Made circa 1867–1902. Quantity totaling over one million.

Remington US Navy Rolling Block Carbine. Circa 1868–1869. Quantity made estimated 5000.
Caliber .50-70 center fire; 23.75–inch barrel.

Remington Number One Rolling Block Sporting Rifles, Various Types. Overall period all types circa 1868–1902.

Remington Model 1867 Navy Cadet Rolling Block Rifle. Made by Springfield Armory circa 1868 utilizing Remington actions only; the same action as the 1868–1869 Navy Carbine. Quantity made, 498.
Caliber .50-45 center fire cadet cartridge; 23.5–inch round barrel.

Remington New York State Contract Rolling Block Rifles and Carbines. Made for New York State National Guard circa 1872. Total quantity estimated at 15,000.
Rifle has 36–inch barrel.

Sporting Rifle Number 1.
Calibers .40-50, .40-70, .44-77, .45-70, .50-45, .50-70; 23–inch and 30–inch octagon barrels.

Long Range 'Creedmoor' Rifle. Made circa 1873–1890. Quantity estimated as a few thousand.
Calibers .44-90, .44-100, .44-105. 34–inch part octagon/part round barrel.

Remington Model 2 Sporting Rifle. Made circa 1873–1910. Exact quantities unknown.
Large variety of rimfire calibers from .22 to .38 as well as center fire from .22 to .38-40; 24–inch and 26–inch octagon barrel standard.

Mid-Range Target Rifle. Made circa 1875–1890.
Calibers .40-70, .44-77, .45-70, .50-70; 28–inch and 30–inch part octagon/part round barrels.

Short Range Rifle. Made circa 1875–1890. Quantity estimated several thousand.
Center fire calibers .38 extra long; .40-50; .44 S&W; .44 extra long. Rimfire calibers .38 extra long; .44 extra long and .46; 26–inch and 30–inch optional octagonal or round barrels.

Black Hills Rifle. Made circa 1877–1882.
Caliber .45-60 center fire; 28–inch round barrel.

Remington-Keene Magazine Bolt Action Rifle. Made circa 1880–1888. Total quantity estimated at 5000.
Caliber .45-70 most widely made and most popular and in demand; also in .40 caliber and .43 caliber. 24.5–inch round barrel standard.

Remington-Hepburn Number 3 Improved Creedmoor. Made circa 1880–1907. Quantity unknown

Remington-Lee Magazine, Bolt Action Rifles. Made circa 1880–1907. Total quantity in excess of 100,000.

Remington-Hepburn Number 3 Long Range Military Rifle. Made circa 1880s; quantity unknown.
Chambered for .44-75-520 Remington straight cartridge; 34–inch round barrel.

Remington-Hepburn Number 3 Sporting and Target Model. Made circa 1883–1907. Quantities unknown, estimated at 8000 to 10,000.
Listed in a tremendous variety of calibers from .22 Winchester center fire to .50-90 Sharps straight. Barrel lengths 26 inches, 28 inches and 30 inches.

These pages, column by column, from top to bottom, starting at left: Four Rifle Canes; a cutaway of the Rolling Block action; Remington Custom shop designs commemorating the millionth Model 742 auto rifle, the two millionth Model 1100 auto shotgun and Remington's overall 10 millionth gun; a Model 742 Woodsmaster autoloading rifle; the Model 742 Woodsmaster BDL Custom Deluxe; the Model 760 Gamemaster; the Model 760 BDL Custom Deluxe; an era-spanning array of six Remington rifle and shotgun models; Model 2 Sporting Rifle; Remington-Hepburn Number 3 Creedmore; Remington-Hepburn Number 3 Sporting Model.

Remington-Hepburn Number 3 Match Rifle. Made circa 1883–1907. Quantity unknown.

Remington Model 1 1/2 Sporting Rifle. Manufactured circa 1888–1897. Estimated several thousand manufactured.

Rimfire calibers .22, .25 Stevens, .25 long, .32, .38 long and extra long. Center fire calibers .32-20, .38-40, .44-40; 24–inch to 28–inch medium weight octagon barrel.

Remington New Model Number 4 Rolling Block Rifle. Made circa 1890–1933. Quantity made estimated at over 50,000.

Chambered for rimfire calibers .22 short, long and long rifle; .25 Stevens; .32 short and long; 22.5–inch octagonal barrels for most production (24–inch also in .32 caliber) with round barrels available in latter years of production.

Remington Number 5 Rolling Block Rifles and Carbine. Made circa 1897–1905. Three basic styles. Total quantity estimated at 100,000.

Remington-Hepburn Number 3 High-Power Rifle. Believed introduced around 1900 and made to circa 1907. Quantity unknown.

Calibers .30-30, .30 Government, .32 Special, .32-40 HP, .38-72; 26–inch, 28–inch and 30–inch round barrels standard.

Remington Number 6 Rolling Block Type Rifle. Made circa 1902–1933. Exact quantities unknown, but over 250,000 or more.

Rimfire calibers .22 short, long, long rifle and .32 short and long; also available in smoothbore for shot cartridges; 20–inch round barrel.

Remington Number 7 Rifle, Rolling Block Action. Made circa 1903–1911.

Rimfire calibers .22 short and long rifle, .25-10 Stevens; 24–inch, 26–inch and 28–inch part octagon/part round barrels.

Remington-Hepburn Number Schuetzen Match Rifle, aka 'Underlever Hepburn,' aka 'The Walker-Hepburn.' Made circa 1904–1907.

Calibers .32-40, .38-40, .38-50, .40-65; 30–inch or 32–inch part octagon/part round barrel.

Remington Model 8A Autoloading Rifle. Made circa 1906–1936.

Calibers .25, .30, .32 and .35 Remington. Standard grade. Takedown. Detachable box magazine holds five cartridges; 22-inch barrel. Weight, 7.75 pounds.

Remington Model 12A Slide Action Repeating Rifle. Made circa 1909–1936.

Caliber .22 short, long or long rifle. Standard grade. Hammerless. Takedown. Tubular magazine holds 15 short, 12 long or 10 long rifle cartridges; 22-inch round barrel. Weight, 4.5 pounds.

Remington Model 14A High Power Slide Action Repeating Rifle. Made circa 1912–1935.

Calibers .25, .30, .32 and .35 Remington. Standard grade. Hammerless. Takedown, five-shot tubular magazine. 22–inch barrel. Weight about 6.75 pounds.

Remington Model Number 4S 'Military Model' Rolling Block Sporting Rifle, aka 'Boy Scout Rifle.' Made circa 1913–1923. Approximate quantity made estimated from 10,000 to 25,000.

Caliber .22 rimfire short and long; 28–inch round barrel.

Remington Model 16 Autoloading Rifle. Made circa 1914–1928. Closely resembles the Winchester Model 03.

Calibers .22 short, .22 long rifle, .22 Winchester rimfire, .22 Remington Automatic. Takedown, 15-shot tubular magazine in buttstock; 22-inch barrel. Weight, 5.75 pounds.

Remington Model 30A Bolt Action Express Rifle. Made from 1921–1940.

Calibers .25, .30, .32 and .35 Remington, 7mm Mauser, 30-06. Standard grade. Modified M/1917 Enfield Action. Five-shot box magazine; 22-inch barrel. Weight about 7.25 pounds.

Remington Model 24A Autoloading Rifle. Made circa 1922-1935.

Calibers: .22 short, .22 long rifle. Standard grade. Takedown. Tubular magazine in buttstock, holds 15 short or 10 long rifle; 21-inch barrel. Weight about five pounds.

Remington Model 241A 'Speedmaster' Autoloading Rifle.
Calibers .22 short, .22 long rifle. Standard grade. Takedown. Tubular magazine in buttstock, holds 15 short or 10 long rifle; 24–inch barrel. Weight about six pounds.

Remington Model 552A 'Speedmaster' Autoloading Rifle.
Caliber .22 short, long, long rifle. Tubular magazine holds 20 short, 17 long, 15 long rifle; 25–inch barrel. Weight about 5.5 pounds.

Remington Model 33 Bolt Action Single Shot Rifle. Made circa 1931–1936.
Caliber .22 short, long, long rifle. Takedown; 24-inch barrel. Weight about 4.5 pounds.

Remington Model 34 Bolt Action Repeating Rifle. Made circa 1932–1936.
Caliber .22 short, long, long rifle. Takedown. Tubular magazine holds 22 short, 17 long or 15 long rifle; 24–inch barrel. Weight about 5.25 pounds.

Remington Model 81A 'Woodmaster' Autoloading Rifle. Made circa 1936–1950.
Calibers .30, .32 and .35 Remington, .300 Savage. Standard grade. Takedown. Five-shot box magazine (not detachable); 22–inch barrel. Weight, 8.25 pounds.

Remington Model 121A 'Fieldmaster' Slide Action Repeating Rifle. Made circa 1936–1954.
Caliber .22 short, long, long rifle. Standard grade. Hammerless. Takedown. Tubular magazine holds 20 short, 15 long or 14 long rifle cartridges. 24-inch round barrel. Weight, six pounds.

Remington Model 141A 'Gamemaster' Slide Action Repeating Rifle. Made circa 1936–1950.
Calibers .30, .32 and .35 Remington. Standard grade. Hammerless. Takedown. Five-shot tubular magazine; 24-inch barrel. Weight about 7.75 pounds.

Remington Model 511A 'Scoremaster' Bolt Action Box Magazine Repeating Rifle. Made circa 1939–1962.
Caliber .22 short, long, long rifle. Six-shot detachable box magazine. Takedown; 25-inch barrel. Weight about 5.5 pounds.

Remington Model 550A Autoloading Rifle. Made circa 1941–1971.
Has 'Power Piston' or floating chamber which permits interchangeable use of .22 short, long or long rifle cartridges. Tubular magazine holds 22 short, 17 long, 15 long rifle; 24–inch barrel. Weight about 6.25 pounds.

Remington Model 521 TL Junior Target Bolt Action Repeating Rifle. Made circa 1947–1969.
Caliber, .22 long rifle. Takedown. Six-shot detachable box magazine; 25–inch barrel. Weight about seven pounds.

Remington Model 721A Standard Grade Bolt Action High Power Rifle. Made circa 1948–1962.
Calibers: .264 Winchester, .270 Winchester, .30-06. Four-shot box magazine; 24–inch barrel. Weight about 7.25 pounds.

Remington Model 722A Standard Grade Bolt Action Sporting Rifle. Made circa 1948–1962. Same as Model 721A, except shorter action.
Calibers .257 Roberts, .308 Winchester, .300 Savage. Weight, seven pounds.

Remington Model 760 'Gamemaster' Standard Grade Slide Action Repeating Rifle. Made circa 1952–date.
Calibers .223 Remington, 6mm Remington, .243 Winchester, .257 Roberts, .270 Winchester, .280 Remington, .30-06, .300 Savage, .308 Winchester, .35 Remington. Hammerless; 22–inch barrel. Weight about 7.5 pounds.

Remington Model 572A 'Fieldmaster' Slide Action Repeater. Made circa 1955–date.
Caliber, .22 short, long, long rifle. Hammerless. Tubular magazine holds 20 short, 17 long, 15 long rifle; 23-inch barrel. Weight about 5.5 pounds.

Remington Model 40X Heavyweight Bolt Action Target Rifle. Made circa 1955–1964. Action similar to Model 722.
Caliber .22 long rifle. Single Shot. Click adjustable trigger; 28–inch heavy barrel. Weight, 12.75 pounds.

Top to bottom, starting with the extreme left column: A New Model Number 4; a Number 5; a Number 7; a Model 8A auto; a Model 14A pump; a Model 4S Boy Scout Rifle; a Model 24A auto; a Model 33 bolt action; a Model 34 bolt action; a Model 141 pump; a Model 760; a Model 760 Deluxe; and a Model 40X.

Remington Nylon 66 'Mohawk Brown' Autoloading Rifle. Made circa 1959–date.

Caliber .22 long rifle. Tubular magazine in buttstock holds 14 rounds. 19.5–inch barrel. Weight about four pounds.

Remington Model 742 'Woodmaster' Automatic Big Game Rifle. Made circa 1960–date.

Calibers 6mm Remington, .243 Winchester, .280 Remington, .30-06, .308 Winchester. Gas-operated semiautomatic. Four-shot clip magazine; 22–inch barrel. Weight, 7.5 pounds.

Remington Nylon 76 Lever Action Repeating Rifle Made circa 1962–1964. Other specifications same as for Nylon 66.

Short-throw lever action.

Remington Model 700ADL Center Fire Bolt Action Rifle. Made circa 1962–date.

Calibers .22-250, .222 Remington, .25-06, 6mm Remington, .243 Winchester, .270 Winchester, .30-06, .308 Winchester, 7mm Remington Magnum. Magazine capacity: six-shot in .222 Remington, four-shot in 7mm Remington Magnum, five-shot in other calibers. Barrel lengths 24–inch in .22-250, .222 Remington, .25-06, 7mm Remington; 22–inch in other calibers. Weight, seven pounds.

Remington Model 660 Bolt Action Carbine. Made circa 1963–1971.

Calibers .222 Remington, 6mm Remington, .243 Winchester, .308 Winchester. Five-shot box magazine (six-shot in .222); 20–inch barrel. Weight, 6.5 pounds.

At top, directly above: A Model 742. Below, from the top down: The Model 74 Sportsman autoloader; the Model 76 Sportsman pump action rifle; and the Sportsman 581 bolt action rifle. At right: The Model LT20 Limited, a milestone marking 60 years of Remington auto shotguns.

Remington Model 600 Bolt Action Carbine. Made circa 1964–1967.

Calibers .222 Remington, 6mm Remington, .243 Winchester, .308 Winchester, .35 Remington five-shot box magazine (six shot in .222 Remington); 18.5–inch barrel with ventilated rib. Weight, six pounds.

Remington Model 40-XB Center Fire Match Rifle. Made circa 1964–date.

Calibers: .222 Remington, .222 Remington Magnum, .223 Remington, .22-250, 6x47mm, 6mm Remington, .243 Winchester, .25-06, 7mm Remington Magnum, .30-06, .308 Winchester (7.62mm NATO), .30-388, .300 Winchester Magnum. Bolt Action single shot; 27.25–inch standard or heavy barrel. Weight, 9.25 pounds heavy barrel.

Remington Model 788 Center Fire Bolt Action Rifle. Made circa 1967–date.

Calibers .222 Remington, .22-250, .223 Remington, 6mm Remington, .243 Winchester, .308 Winchester, .30-30, .44 Remington Magnum. Three-shot clip magazine (four-shot in .222 and .223 Remington); 24–inch barrel in .22s, 22–inch in other calibers. Weights 7.5 pounds with 24–inch barrel, 7.25 pounds with 22–inch barrel.

Remington Model 580 Bolt Action Single Shot Made circa 1967–date.

Caliber .22 short, long, long rifle; 24–inch barrel. Weight, 4.75 pounds.

Remington Model 541-S Custom Sporter Made circa 1972–date.

Caliber .22 short, long, long rifle. Bolt action repeater. Scroll engraving on receiver and trigger guard. Five-shot clip magazine; 24–inch barrel. Weight, 1.5 pounds.

Remington Nylon 66 Bicentennial Commemorative. Made in 1976. Same as Nylon 66, except has commemorative inscription on receiver, celebrating the 200th anniversary of American independence.

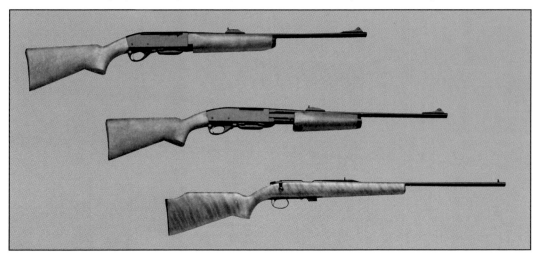

Remington Shotguns

Remington-Whitmore Model 1874 Double Barrel Hammer Shotgun and Rifle. Made circa 1874–1882. Total quantity estimated at a few thousand.

Barrels 28–inch and 30–inch, steel standard.

Model 1882 Double Barrel Hammer Shotgun. Made circa 1882–1889. Total quantity estimated at approximately 7500.

Gauges 10 and 12; 28–inch and 30–inch steel or damascus barrels.

Model 1885, Model 1887, Model 1889 Double Barrel Hammer Shotguns. Made circa 1885–1909. Total quantity unknown, estimated over 30,000.

Gauges 10, 12, 16; barrel lengths 28 inches to 32 inches; available in steel or damascus barrels.

Hammerless Shotguns Model 1894 and Model 1900. Made circa 1894–1910. Total produced unknown.

Gauges 10, 12, 16; barrel lengths from 26 inches to 32 inches, steel or damascus twist.

Remington Model 11A Standard Grade 5-Shot Autoloader. Made circa 1905–1949.

Gauges 12,16 and 20. Hammerless Browning type. Takedown. Tubular magazine holds four shells. Plain, solid rib or ventilated rib barrels; lengths from 26 inches to 32 inches.

Remington Model 10A Standard Grade Slide Action Repeating Shotgun. Made circa 1907–1929.

Gauge, 12. Hammerless. Takedown; six-shot. Five-shell tubular magazine. Plain barrels, 26 inches to 32 inches.

Remington Model 17A Standard Grade Slide Action Repeating Shotgun. Made circa 1921–1933.

Gauge, 12. Hammerless. Takedown. Five-shot. Four-shell tubular magazine. Plain barrels, 26 inches to 32 inches; full, modified or cylinder bore chokes. Weight about 5.75 pounds.

Remington Model 29A Standard Grade Slide Action Repeating Shotgun. Made circa 1929–1933.

Gauge, 12. Hammerless. Takedown. Six-shot. Five-shell tubular magazine. Plain barrels, 26 inches to 32 inches; full, modified or cylinder bore chokes. Weight about 7.5 pounds.

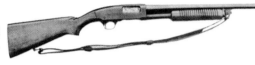

Remington Model 31A Standard Grade Slide Action Repeater.

Gauges 12, 16 and 20. Hammerless. Takedown. Three-shot or five-shot. Tubular magazine holds two or four shells. Plain or ventilated rib barrels; lengths from 26 inches to 32 inches.

Remington Model 32A Standard Grade Over-and-Under Gun. Made circa 1932–1942.

Guage, 12. Hammerless. Takedown. Automatic ejectors. Plain, raised matted solid rib, ventilated rib barrels; 26 inches, 28 inches, 30 inches, 32 inches. Weight about 7.75 pounds.

Remington Sportsman-48A Standard Grade 3-Shot Autoloader. Made circa 1949–1959.

Gauges 12, 16 and 20. Streamlined receiver. Hammerless. Takedown.

Remington Wingmaster Model 870AP Standard Grade 5-Shot Slide Action Repeater. Made circa 1950–1963.

Gauges 12, 16 and 20. Hammerless. Takedown. Tubular magazine holds four shells. Plain, matted top surface or ventilated rib barrels; 26-inch improved cylinder, 28-inch modified or full choke, 30-inch full choke (12 gauge only). Weight about seven pounds.

Remington Sportsman-58ADL Autoloader. Made circa 1956–1964.

Gauge, 12. Deluxe grade. Gas-operated; three-shot magazine. Plain or ventilated rib barrels; 26 inches, 28 inches, 30 inches. Weight about seven pounds.

Remington Model 1100 Automatic Field Gun. Made circa 1963–date.

Gauges 12, 16 and 20. Gas-operated. Hammerless. Takedown. Plain or ventilated rib barrels; 30-inch/full, 28-inch/modified or full, 26-inch/improved cylinder. Weights average 7.25 to 7.5 pounds.

Remington Model 3200 Field Grade Over-and-Under Shotgun. Made circa 1973–date.

Gauge, 12. Box lock. Automatic ejectors. Selective single trigger. 2.75–inch chambers. Ventilated rib barrels: 26-inch improved cylinder and modified; 28-inch, modified and full, 30-inch modified and full choke. Weight about 7.75 pounds.

Top to bottom, left to right: The super fine Remington Special Model 1900, one of the finest doubles ever produced; the Model 17A Standard pump; the Model 31A Standard; and the Sportsman-48A Standard-Grade Autoloader.

Other Remington Products

Remington has been known to make tools and bicycles as well as firearms, ammunition, typewriters and sewing machines! *At right, from the top down:* The Remington Industrial Kiln Gun was an 8 gauge (special shell) single shot breech loader used for firing kilns; the Model 450 Stud Driver used special .32 caliber rimfire rounds for driving studs; and the Model 455 'Double Duty' Stud Driver was for driving thick studs and was convertible from .32 to .22 caliber. *Below:* This prim woman posed for the photographer with Ilion, New York's very first women's bicycle—a Remington product. *At bottom:* This pleasant lady, in a photo from the 1950s, poses with a Remington Model 1897 'commuter' bicycle.

Over the many years since Eliphalet Remington turned out his first rifle in 1816, Remington has introduced more rifles, shotguns, pistols and ammunition than any other manufacturer. All of Remington's products are indeed made in America, as is fitting and proper for one of America's premier firearms manufacturers. Over the years, Remington has introduced many, many epochal innovations—the first successful breechloader and the clip-fed bolt action, to name only two of the myriad inventions with which Remington has contributed to the firearms industry world wide.

'Remington—as American as apple pie.' So implies this homey photograph (below), taken very early on a chilly autumn morning, of a prime example of the improved Model 870 Wingmaster—one of the sporting world's great pump action shotguns, and a carrier of the Remington tradition of unmatched craftsmanship.

Index